Beyond Viagra

Plain Talk About Treating Male and Female Sexual Dysfunction

ALFRED J. NEWMAN, M.D., PH.D.

STARRHILL PRESS
Montgomery

Starrhill Press
P.O. Box 551
Montgomery, AL 36101

ISBN 1-57359-014-2

Design by Randall Williams
Illustrations by Elizabeth Perry
Printed in the United States of America

STARRHILL PRESS IS AN IMPRINT OF BLACK BELT PUBLISHING, LLC, MONTGOMERY, ALABAMA

*The Black Belt, defined by its dark, rich soil, stretches across central
Alabama. It was the heart of the cotton belt. It was and is a place of
great beauty, of extreme wealth and grinding poverty, of pain and joy.
Here we take our stand, listening to the past, looking to the future.*

To my wife, Carolyn,
without whose love, support, and encouragement,
I could not and would not have taken on this task;

and to my patients,
who inspired me to assemble all the latest information,
on both male and female sexual dysfunction,
into one text for patient education.

Acknowledgments

My son Alfred Newman III and his wife, Catherine, were of invaluable help in providing research and finding current references for some of the key topics under female sexual dysfunction.

My brother-in-law Bob Gilliland and his wife, Mary Jo, were of tremendous help in tracking down the most current information through many hours spent on the internet.

My urology practice office staff—Judy, Tina, Tara, Chuck, Jennifer, Fran, and Ann—were very patient with me while I was dividing my time between caring for my patients and working on "the book." Special thanks go to Ann, who typed the manuscript.

Randall Williams is a talented and untiring editor, without whose encouragement, energy, and editorial skills this book could not have been produced, let alone in a very fast summer.

Contents

Figures and Tables

Figs.

Tables

Preface

Since going on sale in April 1998, Viagra has become not just the talk of the town but the talk of the globe. As a urologist with a busy practice, I have treated thousands of impotent men over the past twenty years. I can certify that the wonder drug's immediate impact has been unprecedented in my profession and that it has truly revolutionized the initial approach to the treatment of erectile dysfunction. In the process, the tiny blue pill has fueled new debates over sexuality, medical insurance, government regulation, and even foreign trade.

Viagra does not work in all cases, but the majority of impotent men who take the drug have positive results with few side effects. For now, Viagra has made my job as a urologist much easier. In almost every case, a new patient who comes in with an impotency problem will get a Viagra prescription instead of a lengthy, expensive evaluation involving numerous tests. The patient who does not respond fully to Viagra is then a candidate for a complete work-up and a return to pre-Viagra treatment options. Many people do not understand what those options are, and one of my goals in this book is to explain them.

Viagra is obviously the treatment of the nineties for erectile dysfunction, but there were other significant advances in the sixties, seventies, and eighties. There will be other advances in the future. Thus it is important to remember that no matter how revolutionary and useful it is, Viagra is not the be-all and end-all of impotency treatment.

Also, Viagra does not work by itself. The drug enhances the functioning of the wonderfully complicated process that results in an erect penis, but Viagra does not create or increase desire. As I began thinking about writing this book, I realized that I wanted to discuss Viagra but in the context of overall sexual function and dysfunction.

So, in the chapters that follow, we will look closely at how the penis works. You will be surprised at much of this, and I think you will be fascinated, for the male reproductive system is one amazing piece of engineering. There is some complicated medical information in the first few chapters, but I've tried to explain things so a layperson can understand the summaries and any doctors reading this book will find sufficient detail for their purposes, too. After examining the common causes of male impotency (erectile dysfunction), the current pre-Viagra treatment options are summarized. Then an in-depth look at Viagra is presented: What is it? How do I take it? What are the contraindications? What about side effects? What is the cost? These and other questions are answered.

What about Viagra for females? Viagra does affect women, and answers to these and other questions about future uses of Viagra will be forthcoming from studies currently underway.

As male self-esteem is returned and self-confidence is elevated, will men use Viagra to improve relationships and become more romantic? Only time will tell, yet the potential of Viagra and other erectile dysfunction treatments for improving relationships is one of the most important themes of this book. What's love got to do with it? sings Tina Turner. The answer is . . . a lot.

After thirst and hunger, sex is one of the most basic and powerful human urges. The man who wants to be sexually active but cannot get or sustain an erection may be embarassed to talk about his problem, but most impotent men can be helped. This book shows how.

I've tried to make the book fun and interesting to read. I pass along some of the jokes and quotes I've heard, and I also talk some about the common misconceptions and myths we've heard all our lives about sex in general and the penis in specific. Actually, they're not all myths, but we'll get to that . . .

1

THE MECHANICS

Understanding
Normal Male Sexual Function

T he natural erection is the result of an extraordinarily complex process that mankind understands better after the last thirty years of scientific research. We still don't have all of the answers on the exact role of all components at the molecular level but we have progressed light years from Aristotle, who stated that three branches of nerves carry spirit and energy to the penis and that an erection is produced by the inflow of air.[1] This was the accepted wisdom until 1504, when Leonardo da Vinci noted a large amount of blood in the erect penises of men who had been executed by hanging. This observation deflated the concept of the air-filled penis. Perhaps it also gave rise to the term "well hung." In any case, da Vinci wrote:

> "The penis does not obey the order of its master, who tries to erect or shrink it at will. Instead, the penis erects freely while its master is asleep. The penis must be said to have its own mind, by any stretch of the imagination."

In "erectology" as in many other fields, da Vinci was a genius well ahead of his time. His writings on the subject were kept secret until the 1900s, but many investigators in the last 50 years [2, 3, 4, 5] have stressed the importance of increased blood flow through the arteries *into* the penis.

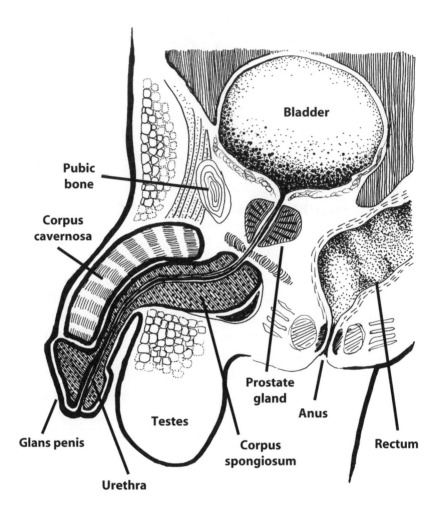

Fig. 1: Overview of the Male Genitalia

Meanwhile, the role of blood flow through the veins *out of* the penis has been controversial. One study shows a small decrease in venous flow.

So how does it really work? Understanding normal erectile function requires a review of the anatomy of the penis [see Fig. 1]. Here and at other points throughout this book, there are some complicated descriptions. I'll give a "plain talk summary" of the information, then I'll go through it again in more medical terms. If you are not a doctor, the summaries may be all you need. Here's the first one:

Plain Talk Summary of Normal Male Sexual Function

A natural erection is the result of a rather complex process. The penis has three separate tubes [see Fig. 2] that become engorged with arterial blood during arousal. Erotic fantasies or sensory inputs such as the touch, scent, sound, or sight of a partner are channeled into the control center in the brain. The aroused brain sends signals down the spinal column to the penile nerves (which may also be directly stimulated by manual stroking of the genitalia or with the act of sexual intercourse itself). The nerve impulses trigger an event involving muscle tissue and blood vessels in the two large erectile cylinders, the *corpus cavernosa*.

There are arteries and spaces called *sinusoids* within these cylinders, and smooth muscle tissue surrounds the arteries and spaces. Normally, the smooth muscle tissue keeps both arteries and spaces constricted, but the nerve impulses send a primary messenger called nitric oxide (NO). This molecule tells the smooth muscle tissue to relax, which allows more arterial blood to flow into the penis and the capacity of the penis to dramatically increase in volume. Meanwhile, veins that normally drain blood from the penis are flattened by the expanding volume of blood into the erection chambers. The arterial blood is thus trapped, making the penis very hard and very erect. Continued stimulation keeps the process going and maintains the erection.

Now, here is a more complex description:

Anatomy of the Penis

The penis is composed of three erectile cylinders [Fig. 2]. A pair of

11

spongy cylinders, the corpora cavernosa, are located side-by-side on top. They join in the midline for about 70 percent of their length — that part of the penis that extends from the body — and continue separately behind the pubic bone where they are anchored to the underside of the pelvic bony structure, the *ischiopubic ramus*. Thus, about 30 percent of the penis is buried in the pelvis behind the pubic bone. This bony anchor is very important for normal penile function. Where the corpora cavernosa merge at about the level of the pubic bone, the midline surface between the two cylinders forms an incomplete septum. This is important in that it allows blood to pass freely from one corporal body to another.

A single *corpus spongiosum* is located below the junction of the two corpora cavernosa [Fig. 2]. This simple tube encloses the *urethra* and at its tip forms the *glans penis,* commonly referred to as the "head" of the penis. The urethra extends from the bladder to the tip of the glans penis.

The spongy erectile tissue within the three cylinders consists of a mass of smooth muscle, often referred to as *trabecular smooth muscle,*

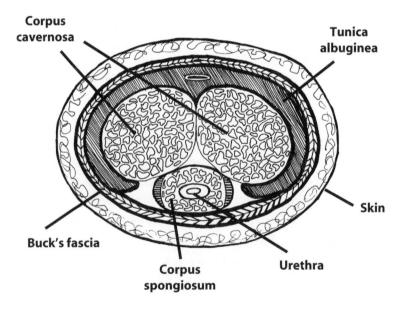

Fig. 2: Cross section of the penis

within which is embedded a network of *endothelial*-lined vascular spaces called sinusoids or lacunar spaces [Fig. 3].[8]

Surrounding each of the corpora cavernosa [Fig. 3] is the *tunica albuginea,* a dense, multilayered, collagenous sheath that gives the penis flexibility, rigidity, and tissue strength.[9] During an erection, one layer of the tunica albuginea stretches lengthways, which allows the penis to become longer, and the other layer stretches crosswise, which allows the penis to become thicker. The third cylinder, the corpus spongiosum, is outside the tunica albuginea and does not become rigid. In addition, all three cylinders are covered by a second, less-dense sheath called *Buck's fascia.*

Penile Blood Supply

Blood supply to the penis originates from the right and left internal pudendal arteries. These arteries are branches of the major blood supply to the pelvis and in turn branch into the deep penile artery that supplies the *corpora cavernosa* through small vessels known as Helisine arteries or arterioles [Fig. 3]. In the flaccid state, the small arterioles are contracted and restrict the arterial inflow into the lacunar spaces. In the erect state, relaxation of the small Helisine arteries allows a rapid increase in blood inflow and exposure of the lacunar spaces (sinusoids) to systemic blood pressure [Fig. 3]. Another branch of the penile artery, the dorsal artery, supplies the glans and the penile skin. The third branch, the bulbourethral artery, supplies the corpus spongiosum.

The most important feature of the venous drainage system is that beneath the tunica albuginea a network of veins, the sinusoidal venules from the lacunar spaces, drains the erectile cylinders when the penis is flaccid. These subtunical venules merge to form emissary venules that exit through the tunica albuginea and pass into the larger venous system, both deep and near the surface.[10] During erection, this network is compressed and stretched by trabecular smooth muscle relaxation [Fig. 3]. The flow of blood in is strong, the flow of blood out is weak, and the result is an erection.

Neurophysiology of Penile Erection

An erection (tumescence) is a neurovascular event, meaning that both the nervous and the circulatory systems are involved. Recent research has identified specific spots in the brain as the integration centers for sexual drive and sexual arousal,[11] perhaps triggered by psychological factors such as erotic fantasies or expectations. Sensory factors such as audiovisual stimulation also have input through these same brain centers. The brain then controls the penis through two kinds of nerves, autonomic [Fig. 4] and somatic.

Autonomic nerves are not controlled by the individual and are "automatic" in their timing and function. There are two types: parasympathetic and sympathetic. The parasympathetic nerve fibers originate from the sacral spinal cord, at levels 2, 3 and 4 (S2-4). The sacral parasympathetic input initiates erections. The sympathetic nerves meanwhile originate from the eleventh and twelfth thoracic levels of the spinal segments, as well as the first and second lumbar spinal segments. This thoracolumbar sympathetic pathway controls detumescence and orgasm. In other words, parasympathetic autonomic nerves get it up; sympathetic autonomic nerves let it down and keep it down [Fig. 4]. As we shall see, complex chemical interactions are involved in this process, which is where Viagra comes into play.

Somatic nerves control sensory and motor functions of the body. Sensory receptors on the glans penis and the penile skin lead to sensory nerves that converge to form the primary dorsal nerve of the penis; this becomes the pudendal nerve which courses up to the sacral segments S2, 3, 4.

As noted above, during an erection the penis is transformed from a venous to an arterial organ.[12] Blood flow into the penis is controlled by three neurotransmitter systems: adrenergic nerve fibers; cholinergic nerve fibers; and nonadrenergic-noncholoinergic (NANC) fibers that release nitric oxide (NO). The exact nerve-chemical processes are very complex. I have included them in a note* on the next page, but I had to reach back to my chemistry doctoral studies to write that section and you

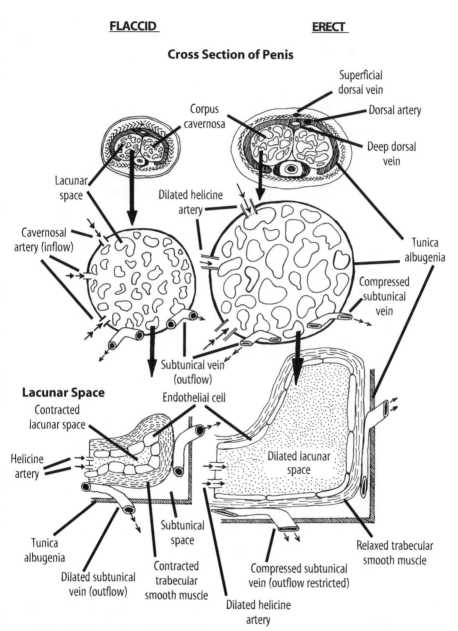

FLACCID   **ERECT**

Cross Section of Penis

Superficial dorsal vein

Dorsal artery

Corpus cavernosa

Deep dorsal vein

Lacunar space

Dilated helicine artery

Cavernosal artery (inflow)

Tunica albugenia

Compressed subtunical vein

Subtunical vein (outflow)

Endothelial cell

Lacunar Space

Contracted lacunar space

Dilated lacunar space

Helicine artery

Tunica albugenia

Subtunical space

Dilated subtunical vein (outflow)

Contracted trabecular smooth muscle

Compressed subtunical vein (outflow restricted)

Dilated helicine artery

Relaxed trabecular smooth muscle

Fig. 3: Vascular Circulation

The left side of the diagram shows the blood flow within the corpus cavernosa of the flaccid penis; the right side shows the same details in the erect penis. During erection, blood outflow is restricted.

will quickly see why I expect most readers to skip those paragraphs. Expressed in its simplest terms, in the body, certain smooth muscle cells (those muscles we cannot control, as opposed to skeletal muscles) respond to chemical signals released by different nerves. In the penis, these chemicals normally keep the penile erectile tissue in the flaccid condition by keeping the smooth muscle cells contracted. But when the conscious or unconscious brain begins to be sexually stimulated, other chemicals are manufactured, which react with the penile erectile tissue (primarily smooth muscle cells) to set up the sequence of events that leads to an erection.

Thus, a series of coordinated vascular events, controlled by autonomic nerves, leads to an erection: relaxation of the smooth muscle in the sinusoids in the corpus cavernosum; increased arterial inflow; and occlusion of the venous drainage from within the erectile spaces. In addition to the vascular components of an erection, there are skeletal-muscular components as well, which are controlled by the somatic (sensory and motor) nerves. These skeletal components play a role in the "rigid erection phase."

You can see the interplay of all these actions in the following summary of the phases of erection:

FLACCID PHASE: When the penis is resting, the trabecular smooth muscle within the corpus cavernosum is contracted and arterial blood inflow is minimal, while venous outflow is quite rapid. The blood pressure in the intracorporal space is therefore low, about 4-6 mm of Hg.

INITIAL FILLING PHASE: The parasympathetic nerve stimulation now relaxes the smooth muscle of the small arteries and arterioles resulting in a four- to tenfold increase of arterial flow into the penis. Simply put, the penis is rapidly filling up with blood. The increased blood volume in the sinusoids initiates the venous occlusion process due to the stretching of the small veins below the tunica albuginea surface. In this initial filling phase there is very little change in pressure within the two corpora cavernosa.

TUMESCENCE PHASE: In this phase the volume of blood progressively increases and the pressure begins to increase inside each corpus

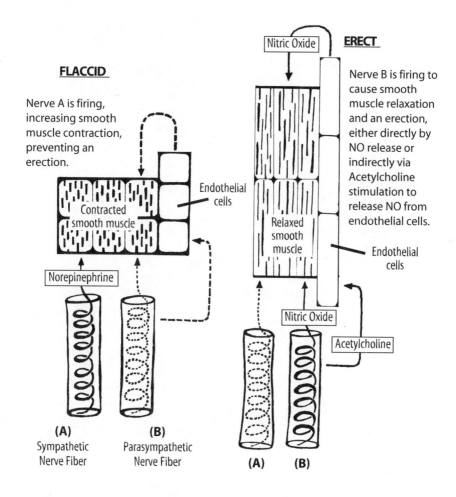

Fig. 4: Nerve Stimulation of Cavernosal Smooth Muscle

This diagram shows the effect of nerve impulses on the endothelial cells and trabecular smooth muscle tissue within the two corpus cavernosum erectile cylinders of the penis. Refer to Figures 2 and 3 for a reminder of where these are located. Again, the left side of the diagram shows the flaccid penis, and the erect penis is on the right. Normally, sympathetic nerves (A) are sending the neurotransmitter norepinephrine to the trabecular smooth muscle tissue, which is contracted. During erection, the parasympathetic nerves (B) send the neurotransmitter Nitric Oxide (NO), which relaxes the trabecular smooth tissue, allowing it to stretch, which allows more blood inflow and simultaneously clamps off the veins which take blood out of the penis. Erection occurs.

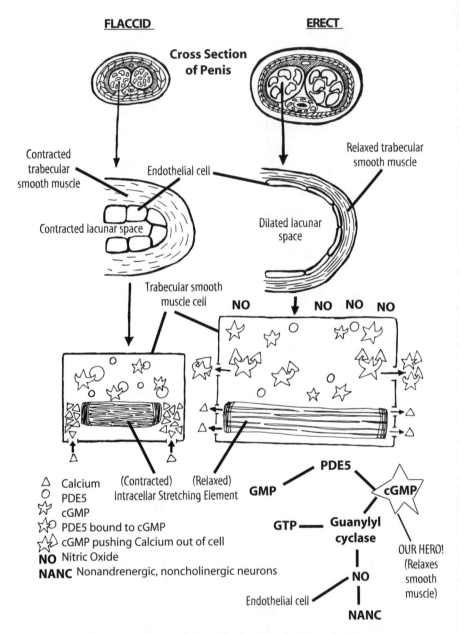

Fig. 5: Biochemistry of Penile Smooth Muscle Tissue

In this diagram, we move from the cross section of the penis (top), to the exploded view of the endothelial cell-lined lacunar space surrounded by the trabecular smooth muscle (center), to the cellular level of the trabecular smooth muscle (bottom).

cavernosum. The clamping down of the small veins below the tunica albuginea continues as the pressure increases. As the overall pressure builds up inside the erectile cylinders, the arterial inflow begins to diminish.

FULL ERECTION PHASE: In this phase the trabecular smooth muscle is fully relaxed and the corpus cavernosum is full with newly infused arterial blood. The arterial inflow is now minimal. The penis is rigid. The venous occlusion mechanism is in full force with no venous drainage. The pressure inside the corpus cavernosum is equal to the average arterial pressure, about 100 mm of Hg.

RIGID ERECTION PHASE: During this phase the pressure inside the corpora cavernosa may temporarily increase to several hundred mm of Hg due to contraction of the pelvic floor muscle outside the penis (ischiocavernosus muscle). Arterial inflow is still zero. The somatic penile nerves, primarily in the engorged, supersensitive glans penis,

---

*Nerve/Chemical Interaction With Erectile Tissue

Adrenergic nerves constrict penile blood vessel and corpora cavernosum smooth muscle via alpah-1 adrenoreceptors. Norepinephrine is the neurotransmitter.[12, 13] Blood vessel and smooth muscle relaxation are controlled by cholinergic (with acetylcholine as a neurotransmitter from parasympathetic nerves) and nonadrenergic-noncholinergic (NANC) fibers. Some of the NANC fibers may contain vasoactive intestinal polypeptide. Vasodilation of the penile vascular structures, from primarily cavernous smooth muscle relaxation, following activation of cholinergic and NANC fibers is mediated by nitric oxide and its second messenger cyclic guanosin monophosphate (cGMP).[13, 14] Second-messenger molecules like cGMP function at the molecular level inside the cell in which they reside, in this case the smooth muscle of the corpora cavernosum [Fig. 5]. We now see that the NANC neurotransmitter nitric oxide (NO) is critical in producing smooth muscle relaxation and penile erection. NO production (synthesis) results from activation of neurogenic and to a small degree, endothelial NO synthase. Once NO diffuses into the smooth muscle cell, it binds to an enzyme guanylyl cyclase [Fig. 5]. This causes an increase in guanylyl cyclase activity, resulting in cyclic GMP (cGMP) production or synthesis. This intracellular second messenger then carries out the final step in relaxing smooth muscle, reducing the level of intracellular calcium [seen schematically in Fig. 5], by binding to cGMP — dependent protein kinases, cGMP dependent ion channels, and cGMP — regulated phosphodiesterases. The overall amount of intracellular cGMP, "man's favorite second messenger," is controlled by and regulated by the activity of the phosphodiesterase 5 (the villain to some), which helps convert cGMP back to GMP. Several other forms of phophodiesterase (PDE) have been identified in penile tissue (types 2, 3, 4 and 5); however, PDE 5 is the predominant phosphodiesterase in human corpus cavernosum and human corpus cavernosa smooth muscle. It also is apparently located just in human penile tissue. Enter Viagra! As we will see in a later chapter, it functions to block PDE 5. This allows cGMP levels to remain high and continue their function as a smooth muscle relaxant that potentiates and maintains the penile erection.

contribute to the sacral nerves to stimulate the pudendal motor nerve which is responsible for contraction of both the ischiocavernosus and bulbocavernosus muscles. A rhythmic contraction of the latter muscle is necessary for ejaculation.

DETUMESCENCE PHASE: Sympathetic (adrenergic) stimulation causes contraction of the trabecular smooth muscle [Fig. 4]. Very rapidly the venous outflow is re-established.[15] The penis then returns to the flaccid phase.

Keep in mind that the major elements of the erection process are occurring in the two erectile cylinders, the corpora cavernosa. During erection, blood flow certainly also increases to the corpus spongiosum tissue around the urethra and to the glans penis. However, the absence of any tunica albuginea in the covering of the glans penis and the presence of only a very thin tunica covering over the corpus spongiosum means there is no significant venous occlusion. Without the thick tunica covering against which the blood veins of the corpora cavernosa are flattened, there is little increased pressure in the glans and in the third penile cylinder. But, during the rigid erection phase, contraction of the ischiocavernosus muscle and bulbocavernosus muscle do compress the spongiosum and penile veins and result in a measurable change in warmth and tone in the head of the penis.

Because men are too often lazy as lovers, the above process could sometimes also be summarized as:

1. Don't bother me till this football game is over.
2. Well, maybe you could sit over here.
3. Hmm, that feels good.
4. Honey, I'm ready.
5. That was great.
6. Zzzzzzz.

WHEN THE PLUMBING FAILS

Overview of Male Sexual Dysfunction

Where men are concerned, the term "sexual dysfunction" can encompass a number of problems with anatomy, physiology, and psychology. Impotence, or the inability to achieve a satisfactory erection, is only one potential problem though it is the one most commonly thought of in relation to male sexual problems. In the United States, some twenty million men are estimated to have some degree of impotence problems. The advent of Viagra has raised awareness of the problem and I expect we will see many more men seeking treatment than in the past. The good news is that noninvasive oral medications can help a large number of these men, and other treatments that have been developed over the past thirty years are constantly being improved and can help many others who do not respond to Viagra.

Sexual dysfunction problem areas that we as urologists see in the office include:

• **PREMATURE EJACULATION.** This is a condition in which the male has an orgasm very quickly following an erection, often even before penetration. The erection may last from a few seconds to a few minutes. The patient complains that he has an uncontrollable ejaculation that always occurs before he wants it to, usually quite promptly after erection. This problem is always psychological in nature. The primary treatment for this condition is consultation with a psychologist who will work with the couple so that the patient can progressively learn better control of the timing of orgasm and subsequent ejaculation. However, in the last ten years we have found several new drugs, mostly antidepressants, whose side effects prolong orgasm or make ejaculation difficult. Therefore, we do have some medications to offer the patient today in addition to consultation with a psychologist who will advise behavior modification protocols.

• INABILITY TO ACHIEVE ORGASM. The rhythmic spasm of the pelvic floor muscles, commonly referred to as an orgasm, is one of the miracles of human existence. An orgasm is actually triggered by a psychological process, occurring at a time when the individual is highly stimulated and excited both physically and emotionally. Thus, when men have difficulty achieving orgasm, the cause is primarily psychological although it certainly can have its basis in certain physical conditions. Diabetics often have a loss of sensation from genital stimulation due to diabetes-induced damage to the nerve fibers, resulting in decreased penile sensation during sex. Therefore, these individuals sometimes have a progressively more difficult time having an orgasm. Patients who have performance anxiety regarding the act of sexual intercourse usually will also have problems having a timely orgasm. At times they may not have an orgasm at all or may simply require an extensive length of time to reach an excitation and sensory level that triggers an orgasm. Even though the orgasm process is primarily triggered by the excitation level of the patient, the end result is contraction of the pelvic floor muscles. Thus, some medicines that act as muscle relaxants can actually make having an orgasm quite difficult. A large number of other drugs, particularly antidepressants, cause major problems with achieving orgasm in both males and females.

• RETROGRADE EJACULATION. This term applies to the event that occurs when the bladder neck is open during ejaculation and the seminal fluid, rather than exiting the end of the penis, instead harmlessly flows into the bladder. During orgasm, the pelvic floor muscles spasm and the seminal fluid, stored in two small glands located behind the bladder, is pushed out into the urethra at a point about two inches downstream from the neck of the bladder. The fluid is then further propelled down the urethra and out the end of the penis by the rhythmic contraction of the pelvic floor muscles. However, patients who have had prostate surgery, testicular cancer surgery, or are diabetic may have damage to some of the pelvic nerves that control and give muscle tone to the neck of the bladder. The emission phase of ejaculation will therefore propel the seminal fluid in a harmless way up into the bladder where it will be emptied the next time the patient urinates. Retrograde ejaculation can also be caused by certain medicines given to patients to relax the bladder neck to offset the effects of an enlarged prostate partially blocking the bladder neck.

• **DECREASED LIBIDO.** This is another problem area very commonly encountered in the practice of urology. Patients who complain of loss of libido frequently have no problem with impotence, just with the sex drive. Male libido is stimulated by the male hormone, testosterone, which is produced in the testicles. At this point there is still a lot of controversy over the exact role of testosterone in producing a normal erection, but it's rather clear that it does have *the* major role in providing for normal sexual desire and sex drive. One of the most common causes of decreased libido therefore is a low testosterone level. Sometimes this is a natural process of aging. On the other hand, patients experiencing significant depression, from whatever causes, invariably will complain of the loss of sex drive. These individuals may have absolutely no problem achieving an erection, but just no desire to do so.

• **IMPOTENCE—ERECTILE DYSFUNCTION.** The urological community refers to impotence as erectile dysfunction, and in this book the two terms are used interchangeably. Urologists currently define impotence as the inability to initiate and maintain an erection adequate for normal intercourse.[16] Obviously, what might be satisfactory erections for one individual might cause a major problem for another. This definition always reminds me of the variability in different cultures around the world as to the sexual prowess expected of the male. In some Middle East countries men are expected to perform with multiple orgasms and multiple erections in one evening. I'm reminded of an

Iranian patient who came to see me about two years ago very distraught over his inability to have "normal" erections. On further questioning, I found that he had recently married an American woman and they were very happy in their marriage except for his obvious disappointment with his ability to perform in the bedroom. His primary complaint was that he could only have one ejaculation per evening and once he had an ejaculation, he had tremendous difficulty obtaining another erection that evening. He was in excellent medical condition and had no evidence of any underlying medical problem to cause any physical problems. The only thing I could tell him was that he must be much more Americanized than he realized because his sexual function was in line with most American males over thirty years of age. Clearly, in the definition of impotence, the degree of difficulty or dissatisfaction with one's erection is in the eye of the beholder, or at least in the mind of the beholder.

However, erectile dysfunction profoundly affects quality of life and is frequently associated with loss of self-esteem, poor self-image, depression, and increased tension with one's sexual partner.[16]

Studies in the United States reveal that erectile dysfunction occurs in 5 percent of men at age forty and increases to 15-25 percent by age sixty-five, although impotence is not an inevitable and untreatable result of aging. For example, the Massachusetts Male Aging Study (MMAS)[17] was a community-based survey of thirteen hundred men aged forty to seventy from 1987 to 1989. Overall, 50 percent had some degree of erectile dysfunction; 10 percent had total loss of erectile function; 25 percent had moderate erectile dysfunction; and 17 percent had mild erectile dysfunction problems. Combining the MMAS data with Census Bureau projections[18] would mean that twenty-five million U.S. men will suffer with erectile dysfunction by 2005.

From the above definition of erectile dysfunction, and from my experience over the past twenty years of treating these problems, I have seen a range of erectile dysfunction that stretches all the way from the patient who can never initiate an erection to the patient who occasionally is unable to maintain an erection quite as long as he would like. This is also the case for the estimated twenty million men in the United States who complain of some degree of erectile dysfunction.[16] This may actually be a low estimate because many patients in the past have been reluctant to tell their primary care physician that they were having difficulty with erectile dysfunction. For the male patient it has always been an important but very difficult step for them to admit that they have this problem and to seek professional help from their primary physician or their urologist. In addition, many health care providers have been reluctant to ask detailed questions about sexual history and sexual function, partly because they may have been misinformed or poorly informed regarding the availability of treatment. Now that we have an effective oral medication, Viagra, that can be prescribed by the primary care physician, hopefully they will be more inclined to ask patients about their sexual history. For today's busy primary care physician, it takes no longer to write a prescription for Viagra, for example, than to write one for other commonly treated problems such as high blood pressure or upper respiratory infections. Along this same vein, as patients are now well aware of Viagra and its benefits, hopefully they will be less hesitant to bring up their problems with erectile dysfunction to their primary care doctor.

Plain Talk Summary

We have seen in this chapter that impotence, now commonly referred to as erectile dysfunction, is defined as the inability to initiate and maintain an erection adequate for normal intercourse. This symptom has the prevalence in the United States today of at least twenty million men. With the availability of the new noninvasive oral medication, Viagra, we expect more men to come forward with this symptom. We have also seen that male erectile dysfunction is just one of several problems that come under the category of male sexual dysfunction. In the next chapter, we will look at the specific causes of erectile dysfunction, and then in the following chapters we will review the various treatments now commonly available.

3

WHY ME?

Causes of Male Erectile Dysfunction

The causes of male erectile dysfunction fall into two general categories: physical (or organic), and psychological. In the early 1970s, psychological impotence was believed to be by far the most common. The noted sex therapy experts Masters and Johnson reported that 90 percent of impotent men suffered from a psychological problem.[19] However, after twenty-five years of advances in the understanding of neurogenic and vascular physiology, we have much better knowledge of the mechanisms of erectile dysfunction. Although the psychological component remains a very important factor in diagnosis and treatment, we now know that at least 80 percent of men who seek medical care for erectile dysfunction will have primary physical problems.[20] On the other hand, it is virtually impossible that impotence, even with an underlying physical cause, won't have an impact on a man's psychological well-being. No one who has failed to initiate or maintain an erection on one occasion can keep from thinking "what if" the erection fails the next time they want to have sexual intercourse.

No matter what the causes of erectile dysfunction, we need to keep in mind the basic principles of the nerve and blood vessel mechanisms discussed in the previous chapters. Factors that tend to prevent initiation of an erection usually involve the nerve supply or can be psychological. Factors that prevent the erectile tissue from fully filling with blood usually have to do with problems of arterial blood flow to the penis. Factors that lead to loss of the erection before orgasm and ejaculation tend to involve failure of the venous occlusive mechanism that, as we have seen, traps blood in the penis and thus maintains the erection. We can easily see that a breakdown in any one of these areas can result in erectile dysfunction.

Most men complaining of erectile dysfunction have at least one, and sometimes several, of the following problem areas: blood flow problems, nerve problems, diabetes, prior surgery, drugs, pelvic trauma or pelvic radiation, Peyronie's disease, and psychological problems.

Blood Vessel Abnormalities

Problems with either the arteries carrying blood to the penis or the veins draining blood from the penis can easily prevent a satisfactory erection. The most common of these problems is blockage of the arteries carrying blood to the penis [see Figure 3]. As we have seen in chapter one, the small arteries carrying blood into the penis at the time of an erection must dilate from five to ten times their normal resting diameter. Even as little as 15 percent occlusion of the small blood vessels is enough blockage to cause a problem.

Such partial arterial blockage is the most common cause of organic impotence and is usually associated with risk factors such as cigarette smoking, diabetes, hypertension (high blood pressure), or even marked elevation of blood cholesterol and fat levels.[20] Other risk factors associated with reduced arterial flow are a history of blunt pelvic trauma or pelvic radiation.[21, 22, 23]

One way to visualize how important it is for these small vessels to dilate and carry more blood to the penis at the onset of an erection is to consider an analogy of a metropolitan water system. The building of a new housing subdivision will result in an increased demand for water. If a water tower already supplies the area, the only way to increase the amount of water flowing from the water tower to the subdivision is to increase the size of the pipes. Simply increasing the height of the water tower or increasing the pressure inside the water tower will not increase the flow of the water to the new subdivision.

The majority of patients who have erectile dysfunction as a result of reduced arterial blood flow will also have more generalized cardiovascular problems throughout the body. Frequently, impotent men also have a history of coronary artery occlusive disease with or without a history of prior heart attacks. Some individuals with erectile dysfunction also have a history of poor blood circulation to their feet and legs, resulting from arterial occlusive disease. Occasionally, we find a patient who has a focal isolated blockage of one of the arteries carrying blood to the penis. This is usually seen in young patients, in their twenties, who have sustained blunt pelvic trauma such as a past pelvic fracture.[23] Diabetic men can have impotence secondary to both effects on the nerve supply to the penis, as well as the vascular supply. Diabetic men, as well as older men, have an increased amount of scarring or fibrosis within the walls of the arteries to the penis. Plaque buildup on these different areas further reduces the inside diameter of the arteries.

Patients with hyperlipidemia, or marked elevation of lipid (fat) levels in the blood, have a definite well-described risk for arteriosclerosis. The extra lipid builds up in the wall of the artery and eventually causes a significant degree of blockage. High blood pressure (hypertension) is another established risk factor for arteriosclerosis. A recent study reported that in one series of impotent men about 45 percent had a history of hypertension.[24] In patients with hypertension, it is not the increased blood pressure itself that contributes to erectile dysfunction. Rather, the associated arterial stenosis found in patients with hypertension is thought to be the cause of the erectile dysfunction.[25]

Failure of the mechanism [See Fig. 3 and Chapter 1] that clamps down on the veins that drain blood from the penis has been proposed as one of the more common causes of vasculogenic impotence.[26] Some men may develop large venous channels that are never quite fully occluded as the arterial blood flows into the penis during the beginning phase of erection. Often, this problem is seen in relatively young patients who have experienced erectile dysfunction over their entire life. Such patients may report relatively normal initiation of an erection, but within a few seconds or up to a minute or so lose the erection without ejaculation. These venous leak-type problems can often be surgically corrected [see Chapter 10].

In Peyronie's disease [see Chapter 12], non-elastic scar tissue forms, primarily along the surface of the tunica albuginea, resulting in inadequate compression of the veins below the tunical surface, therefore preventing entrapment of the arterial blood in the normal fashion.

On the other hand, if the trabecular smooth muscle and the vascular spaces of the penis are unable to relax sufficiently [see Fig. 3], the resulting sinusoidal expansion will be inadequate and the subtunical veins will not be compressed enough to maintain an erection. This may occur in the overanxious individual with excessive adrenergic stimulation. Alteration of the neuro receptors in the smooth muscle may give an adverse response and, in effect, impair relaxation of the smooth muscle in response to the usual nitric oxide stimulation.[27]

Interestingly, cigarette smoking, in addition to causing generalized arterial blockage, may also cause the cavernous smooth muscle to lose its ability to dilate.[28] Again, the net effect is the same—not enough clamping of the penile veins to allow for the heightened intracavernous arterial pressures necessary for an erection.[28] This is yet another reason why one shouldn't smoke in bed, or if one hopes to get into bed.

Neurogenic Problems

Because an erection is a neurovascular event, any disease or trauma that affects the brain, spinal cord, penile nerve supply, or the receptors in the small arteries and cavernous smooth muscle of the penis can lead to impotence.

Without question, diabetes is the single greatest cause of neurogenic erectile dysfunction. Diabetic patients often have peripheral nerve damage that involves various parts of the body. In addition to experiencing decreased function of the nerves leading to the penis, diabetics may exhibit effects on the nerves to the lower extremities and complain of numbness or tingling in their feet. This collection of symptoms is referred to as a peripheral neuropathy. In diabetics, the effect on the nerve supply to the penis is thought to have more to do with erectile dysfunction than the diabetes-related effects of occlusive arterial disease.

Pathologic processes in certain regions of the brain, such as Parkinson's disease, stroke, Alzheimer's disease, brain tumors, and trauma can all result in erectile dysfunction.

Looking specifically at Parkinson's disease, most physicians, myself included, have been unaware of the high incidence of erectile dysfunction in this group of patients. Of the one million patients with Parkinson's in the U.S. today, approximately 600,000 are men, of which some 200,000 have erectile dysfunction. Most Parkinson's sufferers are over sixty, and in men of this age, non-Parkinson's related causes are usually responsible for their erectile dysfunction. However, in those 15 percent of men under age fifty who have Parkinson's (some 30,000 men), the erectile dysfunction is usually caused by the Parkinson's. More importantly, erectile dysfunction may be the first symptom of Parkinson's disease, a fact often appreciated only in retrospect.

Recent personal cases have brought this important fact to light in my practice. Thus, any middle-aged male who has erectile dysfunction and has no other medical problems or risk factors for impotence, who has "slowed down" recently, should be worked up for Parkinson's disease. The main cause of erectile dysfunction in Parkinson's patients is autonomic nervous system insufficiency. Since Parkinson's patients also lose noradrenaline cells in the brain, in addition to the well-documented dopamine cells, this leads to a failure of the autonomic nervous system to help constrict the veins draining the erectile tissue, thus preventing a full erection.

In looking at spinal cord injury patients, the degree of erectile dysfunction depends on the degree of the injury as well as the location. Patients with high spinal cord injuries may still have a reflex erection.

Chronic long-standing alcoholism can result in the loss of an adequate number of neurotransmitters in the penile nerves. This usually takes a very significant amount of alcohol intake over a long period of time—years, not a lost weekend. Another common source of neurogenic-related impotence is found in patients who have had radical prostate cancer surgery, which will be discussed more fully in the section on prior surgery.

Endocrine Disorders

The most common endocrinologic cause of impotence is diabetes mellitus. This disorder, as we have seen, does not cause impotence directly through any resulting hormonal deficiency, but from its effects on the vascular and neurological, as well as psychological components. In patients with chronic diabetes, we can expect from 30 to 70 percent of diabetic males to be affected with erectile dysfunction, due to the effect of the disease on both blood vessels and nerves.

The primary male hormone testosterone is produced in the testicles and is responsible for male sex drive, libido, as well as growth of facial hair and genital hair. At best, testosterone may enhance an erection, but it has been clearly shown that it is not essential for an erection. Most men with low serum testosterone levels who have erectile dysfunction report very little effect of testosterone therapy on their erections.[29, 30] On the other hand, a few men with normal or low normal testosterone levels will report improved erections with testosterone treatment. This is likely due the placebo effect of the testosterone injection or to a more positive feeling of well-being that allows for reduction in performance anxiety.

Hyperprolactinemia, which is an elevated blood level of prolactin, whether as result of a benign pituitary gland tumor or of drugs, will lead to male sexual dysfunction. The symptoms include both the loss of sex drive and erectile dysfunction. Hyperprolactinemia is associated with a low circulating level of serum testosterone. The elevated prolactin appears to inhibit secretion of the gonadotropin-releasing hormone, LH, necessary for testicular production and release of testosterone.[31]

In addition, erectile dysfunction may be associated with both of the common hypothyroid conditions: hypothyroidism (decreased thyroid gland function) and hyperthyroidism (elevated thyroid gland activity).

Prior Surgery

Certain surgical procedures can interfere with both the arterial blood supply and the nerve supply to the penis. By far, the most common operation resulting in erectile dysfunction today is the radical treatment of prostate cancer. Before 1983, reports of postsurgical erectile dysfunction problems after a radical prostatectomy ranged from 60 to 85 percent.[32] In 1983, Walch and his colleagues[33] reported a new technique for radical prostate cancer surgery, designed to avoid injury to branches of the pelvic nerves that lead to the corpora cavernosa. By using this nerve-sparing technique, surgeons have reduced the number of patients who will experience post-surgery erectile dysfunction to a range of 15 percent (in very select patients with small tumors) to 30 percent.[34, 35, 36]

However, this modified surgical technique is limited to use with patients who have an isolated lesion involving just one side of the prostate gland. In that instance the nerves and blood vessels that are protected are those located on the opposite side of the prostate from the location of the cancer. Unfortunately, prostate cancer usually involves both sides of the prostate. Therefore, most patients going into that operation are not candidates for the nerve-sparing technique, because it is very easy to leave tumor behind if the cancer is located close to the nerve bundle on either side of the prostate. Catelona and Associates[37,] among others, have questioned the efficacy of the nerve-sparing procedure to fully eradicate prostate cancer. Therefore, the true incidence of erectile dysfunction following radical prostate cancer surgery varies from as low as 15 percent of those individuals with isolated nodules who are candidates for and receive the nerve-sparing procedure, up to 60 to 85 percent of those who are not candidates for the modified technique. Unfortunately, most patients fit into that 60-85 percent risk for impotence from post radical prostatectomy.

One of the most common operations performed by a urologist is still the transurethral resection of the prostate (TURP) for removal of obstructing prostate tissue. Over the years, the incidence of erectile dysfunction following this procedure has ranged from none[38] to 13 percent.[39]

Patients undergoing surgical reconstruction of the abdominal and pelvic blood vessels may have significant incidence of erectile dysfunction. Most of the underlying erectile dysfunction probably stemmed not from the surgery itself, but rather from the generalized atherosclerosis of not only the abdominal and pelvic vessels but also the small vessels leading to the penis. In fact, in some instances following the vascular procedures, the erectile dysfunction improves. In one report[40], aortofemoral bypass surgery was associated with only a 6 percent erectile dysfunction incidence in previously potent males, while 30 percent of the men who had a mild problem with erectile dysfunction before surgery developed a significant problem afterwards.

In the past, certain operations on the gastrointestinal tract have been associated with high incidents of erectile dysfunction. Surgery for benign inflammatory-type problems involving the colon and rectum have been reported to result in only a 3 percent incidence.[41] On the other hand, surgery for cancer of the rectum, which often involves an operation called "abdominoperineal resection"—surgery both at the level of the rectum and a simultaneous abdominal incision—has been reported to result in erectile dysfunction in about 60 percent of the patients in one series.[42]

Drug-Related Erectile Dysfunction

A large number of therapeutic drugs may have an undesired side effect of erectile dysfunction [see Table 1].[43, 44] While the mechanics causing the problem with the individual drugs are mostly unknown, we are able to reverse the effects of most of these drugs once they are discontinued. This is not necessarily the case for chronic substance abuse of alcohol, marijuana, codeine, heroin, and nicotine.

Nor have we figured out how to mitigate the negative side effects of some drugs contributing to erectile dysfunction even when we know the mechanics involved. For example, some drugs used to suppress tremor in Parkinson's patients, such as benztropine (Cogentin) and trihexyphenidyl (Artane), do so by blocking acetycholine in the brain. When they block acetycholine, the key initiator of nitric oxide release from the endothelial cells of the erectile tissue [Fig. 4] in the autonomic nervous system, then erectile dysfunction occurs. Other drugs used by Parkinson's patients that frequently cause or aggravate erectile dysfunction include the anticholinergic drugs, the tricyclic anti-depressants with anticholinergic activity, antihistamines, alcohol, and beta-blockers.

Pelvic Trauma

Blunt pelvic trauma can result in erectile dysfunction in one of several ways. Individuals who have had deceleration injuries, such as falling off a telephone pole or being hit by a car, frequently have significant long- and short-term damage to the urethra. When that type of injury is surgically repaired and the patient is fully recovered from the trauma, they frequently have a major problem with erectile dysfunction from all of the damage to the nerve and blood supplies to the penis. In those same patients who sustained blunt pelvic trauma, frequently the result is a pelvic bony fracture where the pelvis bone is fractured in three different places and the subsequent damage to the blood vessels in the pelvis results in a large amount of bleeding into the pelvis. This collection of blood (hematoma) ultimately will result in a lot of fibrosis and scarring that again damages the blood and nerve supplies to the penis.

Pelvic Radiation

Another alternative to radical prostate surgery for those patients with localized prostate cancer is radiation therapy. Reports show that from 0 up to 10 percent of patients will sustain erectile dysfunction side effects following radiation therapy to the prostate.[45] Other studies have shown a higher incidence of erectile dysfunction in individuals treated with external beam radiotherapy for prostate cancer. One such study[46] showed that fifteen out of sixteen patients treated with external beam radiation therapy complained afterwards of some degree of erectile dysfunction. Some of the earlier studies may not have assessed the degree of erectile dysfunction preoperatively and therefore have projected a higher actual increased incidence of erectile dysfunction after radiation than actually was the case. We know that up to 20 to 30 percent of patients receiving therapy for prostate cancer have a significant degree of erectile dysfunction prior to the radiation.

The most common source of erectile dysfunction in patients receiv-

Table 1: Drugs that May Produce Erectile Dysfunction

Antihypertensives (for treatment of high blood pressure)
Methyldopa (Aldomet)
Clonidine (Catapress)
Reserpine (Hydropres)
B-Blockers
Guanethidine
Verapamil (Calan)

Diuretics
Thiazide Diuretics
(Hydrochlorthiazide)
Spironolactone (Aldactone)
Hydralazine

Antidepressants
Prozac
Lithium
Monoamine Oxidase Inhibitors
Tricyclic Antidepressants

H₂ Antagonists (to reduce stomach acidity)
Cimetidine (Tagamet)
Ranitidine (Zantac)

Tranquilizers
Phenothiazines
Butyrophenones

Antipsychotics
Chlorpromazine (Thorazine)
Pimozide (Orap)
Thiothixine (Navane)
Thioridazine (Mellaril)

Sulpiride
Haloperidol (Haldol)
Fluphenazine (Prolixin)

Cardiac
Clofibrate
Gemfibrozil
Diagoxin

Hormones
Estrogens
Progesterone
Corticosteroids
Proscar
Eulexin
Casodex
Gonadotropin-releasing
hormone agonists — Zoladex
and Lupron

Cytotoxic Agents
Cyclophosphamide (Cytoxan)
Methotrexate
Roferon-A

Misc.
Baclofen
Tobacco
Alcohol
Amphetamines
Metoclopramide
Opiates
Anticonvulsants
Cocaine
Nonsteroidal antiinflammatory
Ketoconazole (Nizoral)

ing pelvic radiation for prostate cancer has been vasculogenic in origin.[46]

Peyronie's Disease

Peyronie's disease usually manifests itself as a curvature deformity of the penis. Dr. Peyronie first published a report on a collection of patients with this condition in 1743. The disease is thought to involve about 1 percent of adult males, although in some impotency clinics Peyronie's patients account for about 3 percent of the patients seen each year with erectile dysfunction.

An intense inflammatory reaction usually leads to a lot of penile scarring and fibrosis and ultimately to a layer of gristle-like tissue that is easily felt on examination. The fibrosis occurs usually along the top of the two erectile cylinders (the corpus cavernosae), thus preventing their natural stretch and elongation during the normal erection. Meanwhile, the opposite sides of the erectile cylinders are usually not affected and thus stretch in their usual manner. This difference in stretching of the walls of the erectile cylinders of the penis results in the curve, either upward or to the left or to the right. Some patients have such severe curvature that intercourse is impossible. At other times, the patients have both a curvature problem and a problem with erectile dysfunction. We don't know precisely what causes this problem. The common theories include frequent chronic irritation, penile trauma including traumatic intercourse, inherited traits, and autoimmune defects. The trauma to the penis may be from vigorous intercourse, constriction rings, self-injection protocols, or even traumatic catheterization of the bladder.

The acute inflammatory phase, which can last from nine to twelve months, often causes pain with erections, making intercourse very uncomfortable. On the other hand, many patients never report pain with this early stage.

Current understanding of the mechanism of erectile dysfunction in Peyronie's disease suggests that it is a veno-occlusive problem. The fibrous plaque impairs the tunica albuginea in its role as a veno-occlusive organ; the net effect is that the small subtunical venules are not compressed sufficiently, and blood drains from the corpora cavernosae and prevents the storage of blood in the erectile cylinders. Some patients have fibrosis involving not only the surface covering the erectile cylinders, but also the space in between the blood vessels inside the erectile space. This, in effect, may prevent the expansion of the vascular spaces. Other patients have a palpable, firm plaque on the top of the penis without any specific symptoms of impotence or any deformity.

Specific treatments for this condition are discussed in Chapter 12.

Chronic Illness

A large number of systemic chronic diseases and illnesses cause erectile dysfunction by affecting the vascular, neurological, hormonal, or psychological mechanisms. Chronic peripheral vascular occlusive disease, high blood pressure, and diabetes mellitus are among those predisposing factors for erectile dysfunction that have been touched on earlier in this chapter.

In one report,[47] about 60 percent of men suffering from scleroderma, a vascular disease of the skin, exhibited small artery lesions that decreased blood supply to the penis. Chronic renal failure has been reported to cause erectile dysfunction in up to 40 percent of men affected.[48] Erectile dysfunction may affect as many as 50 percent of the patients with alcohol-induced cirrhosis of the liver.[49]

The AIDS epidemic has brought us terrifying images of chronic illness and death among the young and at the same time a characteristic neuropathy develops, which includes neurogenic erectile dysfunction.[50,51]

Loss of erection was reported in 53 percent of a group of fifty-five male Alzheimer's disease patients. This group had a mean age of 70 years[52] but interestingly did not show a correlation between the degree of erectile dysfunction and the degree of cognitive impairment, age, or degree of depression.

Chronic obstructive lung disease, emphysema, has also been reported to be associated with erectile dysfunction.[53] A large number of patients with this problem are chronic cigarette smokers and one would suspect the mechanism to be related to vascular disease, but in this report this group of patients had no higher incidence of vascular disease, as assessed by ultrasound examination of their peripheral pulses. This study suggested that the pulmonary disease itself may be the primary etiologic factor.

Other chronic problems, such as anorexia nervosa, have resulted in erectile dysfunction associated with the neurological complications. The erectile dysfunction symptoms in one group of patients were reversed by treating their electrolyte and fluid deficiency.[54]

Men suffering from depression may have erectile dysfunction secondary to decreased testosterone levels,[55] caused by elevated levels of an endocrine factor (corticotropin-releasing factor). Interestingly, the treatment of this condition with antidepressive drugs sometimes worsens the erectile dysfunction.

Psychological Erectile Dysfunction

Most men with erectile dysfunction have an underlying problem that may be either predominantly psychological or predominantly physical. Men under age thirty-five usually have a predominantly psychological component to their erectile dysfunction. As we saw early on, sexual behavior and the penile erection are controlled primarily by the brain. Specifically, the hypothalamus, the limbic system, and the cerebral cortex are the areas of the brain involved. From these central areas in the brain, either stimulatory or inhibitory messages may be relayed to the spinal erection centers where they either facilitate or inhibit the erection process.

While the exact mechanism of psychological dysfunction has not been established, there are two popular proposals to explain the inhibition of the erection in psychological dysfunction. The first mechanism proposes direct inhibition of the spinal erection center by the brain as an exaggeration of the normal brain inhibition mechanisms.[56] The second proposal suggests excessive sympathetic outflow or elevated peripheral catecholamine levels, which may increase penile smooth muscle tone, thereby preventing the normal relaxation necessary for the erection. Studies in animals have demonstrated that activation of sympathetic nerves or sympathetic infusion of the sympathetic neurotransmitters (epinephrine or norepinephrine) causes detumescence of the erect penis.[57, 58] Clinical studies have shown high levels of blood norepinephrine in patients with psychological erectile dysfunction compared either to normal controls or even to patients in whom vascular disease causes their erectile dysfunction.[59] In general, patients with psychological erectile dysfunction respond most of the time to injection of vasoactive drugs. In those patients with no evidence of vascular and neurogenic disorders, who most likely have primarily psychological erectile dysfunction, an increased central sympathetic tone may therefore be one of the causes of psychological erectile dysfunction, and explains why some of these patients respond poorly to injection therapy.

On a clinical basis, psychological erectile dysfunction has been grouped into four different subgroups.[60] The first group includes those individuals with anxiety and a large amount of fear of failure. This includes individuals with widower's syndrome, sexual phobia, and performance anxiety. Another subgroup includes patients with depression. The depression may be either drug-induced or related to a drug dependency or disease-induced depression. A third subgroup includes those males with marital conflict and individuals with major problems with a very strained relationship. A fourth subgroup includes males with misinformation or lack of information about normal anatomy and male sexual function and the effects of aging on sexual function. These individuals frequently are grouped into the category of those with unrealistic expectations. A fifth subgroup of psychological erectile dysfunction includes individuals with psychiatric problems, including psychotic disorders and obsessive-compulsive personality disorders.

Life Happens: More Psychological Factors

Many stressful life situations can cause erectile dysfunction during the course of a man's life. Fortunately, most such problems are temporary and the problem of erectile dysfunction improves as the precipitating event recedes into the past. Life events that may affect erectile function in the male can be grouped into three general categories depending on the area of their primary impact: A man's sense of masculinity, the marital/partner relationship, and relationships with others.

• **Man's Sense of Masculinity.** A strong sense of masculinity is certainly a prerequisite for satisfactory sexual function in men. What is required to make one feel masculine varies from man to man as do events in life that undermine that sense of masculinity.

With so much emphasis today on health, sports, and the macho image, many men feel inadequate unless they can be nearly perfect physical specimens for their age. Therefore, any deterioration in their physical condition from either a serious, possibly life-threatening illness, such as a heart attack or automobile accident or even a minor sprained muscle, has the potential to produce a devastating effect on a man's erectile function. Even the "weekend warrior" amateur athlete-type injuries may throw a man's sexuality for a loop.

Erectile dysfunction problems may also appear when injury, illness, or death strikes a spouse/partner, parent, friend, or close public figure. These events may trigger brooding thoughts over one's own ultimate physical deterioration and eventual demise, especially if the person who has been stricken is a close contemporary or a role model who has been seemingly invulnerable.

Success in a job or career is very basic to most mens' sense of well-being and masculinity. Being passed over for a promotion, not getting an expected raise, or being fired or demoted may have a significant effect on erectile function. At other times, more subtle changes in the workplace, including new bosses or colleagues or subordinates, may affect erectile function when these changes suggest an upcoming change in the status quo. Even positive events such as a job promotion may trigger concerns of adequately meeting more demanding responsibilities, which can translate into erectile dysfunction.

Retirement can be a very stressful time. Men who mourn the loss of their careers are particularly vulnerable to the development of sexual problems. Since most men's self-esteem comes largely from their work, even those individuals who look forward to retirement may experience problems. Without the daily routine of work, a man may feel stripped of his prestige, identity, significance, and power. At this time a man may also believe that his wife, knowing he now has more time for her, will expect more of him in general, and particularly of his services as a lover. If a man was sexually insecure prior to retiring and had used his work as an excuse for less than inspired lovemaking, his perception of increased expectations may lead to more erectile dysfunction.

A financial reversal may easily have a profound impact on a man's sexual function, since monetary success, or the lack of it, is a measure of a man's worth in today's culture. Setbacks in the financial arena can adversely affect self-perception, add to marital stress, and put strain on relationships with others.

Erectile dysfunction frequently emerges during episodes of Post-traumatic Stress Disorder (PTSD). In this setting, the man often blames himself for being powerless either to prevent the event or to deal with it effectively. For our peace of mind and general well-being, we have to realize that we aren't Rambo, James Bond, or any of the other superheroes whose portrayals in movies and television create unrealistic expectations of how men respond to crises.

• **Marital Stress.** Any number of factors that put stress on the marital relationship can contribute to sexual dysfunction in both men and women. We are speaking in this chapter, of course, about men, but stress is stress regardless of gender. Also, we are speaking generally here about sexual relationships between marital partners, which is the most common situation that physicians like myself see in our practices. However, the basic facts and situations discussed obviously apply to relationships outside the traditional marriage as well.

Here are a number of partner-related factors that can adversely affect a man's erections:

Post-cohabitation erectile dysfunction: Often, the first incident of erectile difficulty occurs when a man and his partner decide to marry after living together happily and successfully for a long time. For some men, this event marks the end of a carefree life and the beginning of a commitment to an anxiety-provoking relationship.[61]

Pregnancy: Some men fear that their own sexual desires can be dangerous when their wife is pregnant. They exaggerate the potential harm of intercourse to the wife and future baby. Becoming a new father can also trigger erectile difficulties. Completely changed household schedules and a likely decrease of privacy and shared social activities frequently add to the potential for erectile dysfunction.

Marital fights: It should surprise no one that arguments with one's sexual partner frequently precipitate erectile problems.

Sexually assertive wife: When the wife becomes more sexually assertive and asks her husband to be a better lover, he may feel threatened. Her behavior usually follows some event(s) that reveals what she may have been missing sexually. For example, she may have read an article or book, talked with a friend, or a professional, or seen a program on television. The husband may react to his wife's increased sexual expectations by worrying that he can no longer satisfy her. And the more he worries about performance, the more likely it is that such anxiety will become a self-fulfilling prophecy of sexual dysfunction.

Extramarital Affairs: When the husband has had an extramarital encounter he may feel guilty, anxious, or depressed and subsequently lose erectile capacity. Some men may fear that their infidelity will become obvious to the wife during intercourse. On the other hand, a wife's affair may be a blow to the husband's ego and a threat to their relationship, particularly as the husband invariably believes that his wife's lover's sexual skills exceed his own. The risk of sexually transmitted diseases from outside relationships is additional fear that can serve as a powerful deterrent to sex, with erectile dysfunction occurring as a common and predictable consequence.

Death or Divorce: The loss of one's wife due to death or divorce often produces erectile difficulties that may not become apparent until the man actually acquires a new partner. Then, the widower may have unanticipated ambivalent feelings about resuming intercourse. On the one hand, he wants to resume sexual activity and get on with his life. At the same time, he may believe he is betraying his deceased wife and disrespecting her memory by having sex with another woman. He may also experience performance anxiety that he and his new partner may not be sexually compatible. Divorce can cause a separate set of problems. If one of the conflicts with his ex-wife was sexual, a man will almost certainly approach sex with a new partner with hesitation, worried that a similar sexual conflict will emerge. In addition, some divorced men may develop a strong set of mixed feelings toward women in general and have ambivalence toward any new potential partner, predisposing them to erectile dysfunction.

• **Relationships With Others.** Erectile dysfunction may follow acute problems with other family members.

Adolescent children: Conflict with teenage children is among the common life events that lead to erectile problems. The conflict may completely preoccupy the father, blocking the relaxation that is necessary for satisfactory sexual function. Even where there is no conflict, when older children return home for holidays, empty-nest parents who have become accustomed to total privacy may find sexual activity more difficult. Fortunately, erectile problems of this nature are usually reversed when the little darlings leave.

Adult children: More significant difficulty may arise when a grown child returns to live at home. The mere presence of the child may cause sexual inhibition, or secondly, the circumstances which led to the child's return often may be distressing of themselves.

Elderly parents: When an older parent comes to live with a couple, the couple's sexual relationship may suffer from the disruption of established family habits and also possibly from stress over the role reversal in which the older parent has become like a "child."

Of course, the above discussion includes only some of the multitude of life events that can precipitate erectile dysfunction. Many of the erection problems described in this section will disappear over time, depending on the severity of the trauma of the triggering event. Up to a month may be required for return of erectile function following a relatively minor traumatic event. On the other hand, following a major traumatic event, up to six months may be required for return to normal erectile function.

Plain Talk Summary of Erectile Dysfunction — Impotence

We have seen in this chapter a large number of potential causes of male erectile dysfunction. Diabetes, with its effects on both the nerve supply and vascular supply to the penis, is probably the leading single contributor. Vascular problems are very common, as well. We have seen how just a small percent (15 percent) occlusion of the small arteries leading to the penis may cause an effective blockade of the arterial filling phase by preventing the five- to tenfold increase in the width of the small blood vessels required for adequate increased arterial flow. Understanding the mechanism as best we can of how certain medications, as well as pelvic trauma or radiation or prior surgery, affects both the nerve supply and vascular supply to the penis helps us understand how we go about evaluating an individual who complains of erectile dysfunction. In the next chapter, we will see how important a good understanding of these causes and their mechanism of impingement on the erectile function, is to the collection of an accurate history and to the completion of a detailed physical exam. We have also seen that while everyone with a physical cause to their erectile dysfunction has a significant impairment of their normal psychological well-being, the vast majority of patients over age forty (about 80 percent) have a primarily physical cause to their erectile dysfunction. On the other hand, patients under age forty frequently have a psychological cause behind their complaints of erectile dysfunction.

4

Doc, I've Got a Problem

Evaluating the Male
With Erectile Dysfunction

As with any other medical problem, evaluation of the patient who has complaints of erectile dysfunction begins with a comprehensive medical and psychosexual history, physical examination, and focused laboratory testing.

The psychosexual history is the most important part of the diagnostic evaluation. A detailed history will help uncover contributory factors to the patient's problem. Knowing that diabetes is a common cause of erectile dysfunction, the first question often asked of the patient is, "Are you a diabetic?" From that point, the questions regarding the patient's past medical history are focused on those items listed in the previous chapter that commonly contribute to impotence.

For example, it's important to know about any and all medications and about any history of heart attacks, carotid artery surgery, or lower extremity vascular surgery. Early in the history-taking, I like to find out if the patient smokes. The number of packs of cigarettes smoked per day multiplied times the number of years smoking equal a number we call "pack years." For example, a patient who has smoked 20 pack years may have enough occlusive disease to partially block the blood flow in the small arteries leading to the penis, which ultimately results in erectile dysfunction. This scenario frequently explains why an otherwise healthy

40-year-old male smoker can have an underlying physical cause to his erectile dysfunction although if he were a non-smoker we would look first for psychological causes.

As we saw in the previous chapter, any prior pelvic surgery, particularly radical prostate cancer surgery, is very important. Questions concerning the patient's libido are very important. Frequently, patients will have severe erectile dysfunction but normal sex drive. These individuals would be expected to have a normal serum testosterone level. On the other hand, some patients report significantly diminished libido, which may be primarily due to a low testosterone level. Or, the lack of sex drive may be affected by an underlying physical cause, resulting in erectile dysfunction, which results in a fear of failure, which results in the patient subconsciously avoiding a situation where they might fail.

As we can see, the urologist's evaluation process begins with a very thorough medical and psychosexual history. The history then guides the subsequent physical examination and any lab tests that are indicated. With a patient with erectile dysfunction complaints, as stated earlier, psychosexual history is probably more important than the medical history. While the medical history helps identify risk factors that contribute to an underlying physical etiology — for example, smoking, history of elevated cholesterol, history of hypertension, or history of previous radical prostate cancer surgery — the psychosexual history helps in determining whether the patient's problem is primarily physical or whether it is primarily psychological. It is very helpful to involve the patient's partner early in the evaluation process. This allows for a very accurate psychosexual history along with good communication and a better therapeutic alliance with the patient.

A number of male sexual function profile questionnaires have been developed in the last ten years. These further help distinguish between psychogenic and non-psychogenic erectile dysfunction. For example, a recent questionnaire (Brief Male Sexual Function Inventory for Urology)[56] includes questions on libido, quality of erection, ejaculation, and the patient's perception of problems in each of the above areas, along with an evaluation of overall satisfaction. These questionnaires are particularly useful in clinical trials where one wants to compare pre- and post-treatment satisfaction levels, regardless of the type of treatment being investigated.

On the other hand, several key questions help more than any others in determining whether the patient's problem is primarily psychological. First, it's helpful to know if the patient still has early morning erections. All normally functioning males should have two or three erections when they are in the deep relaxed REM (Rapid Eye Movement) sleep phase. When Dr. Brantley Scott, who was the leader in developing penile implant surgery as we know it today, was on the Phil Donahue show in 1981, the topic of nighttime penile erections (tumescence) came up. Upon learning that the normal male should have two or three normal erections at night while they are sleeping, Phil Donahue commented, "No wonder we men are so tired when we get up in the morning." Humor aside, when a patient has normal early morning erections but can't perform any other time, there is an excellent chance he has a lot of performance anxiety.

Another key question to sort out physical from psychological under-lying factors regards ejaculation. We ask patients who are having diffi-culty initiating and maintaining an erection if they can still ejaculate with a less than fully erect penis. If the patient can still ejaculate with a somewhat flaccid penis, this implies that his underlying erectile dysfunc-tion problem is physical. If the patient's problem were primarily psycho-logical, he would not only have problems with erectile dysfunction, he would also have problems with achieving orgasm, which depends heavily upon excitation levels and is very easily affected by any degree of performance anxiety.

A classic example where the history helps identify a psychological problem involves the individual with multiple partners. When the male patient gives a history of having no difficulty achieving and maintaining a normal erection with one partner, but has tremendous difficulty with a second partner, the problems with the second partner obviously are not physical.

A history of any underlying psychological conflict in the relationship between the patient and his partner would also be very helpful in establishing whether the problem is primarily psychogenic. A history of performance anxiety from the onset of the relationship with a long history of relationship problems weighs heavily towards the erectile dysfunction being primarily psychological. Determining whether the symptoms of erectile dysfunction have developed gradually over several years or acutely over a matter of several days is also helpful. Patients with a physical problem frequently have a history of gradual decline in their ability to initiate and maintain normal erections, whereas individuals with underlying psychological problems often will have a relatively acute or abrupt onset of symptoms.

As we can see, understanding the mechanism of the normal erection and some of the common causes that contribute to erectile dysfunction by either affecting the arterial blood supply, neurological function, or hormonal function allows the examiner a chance to focus the questions to obtain a thorough and helpful medical and psychosexual history.

The physical exam in general is important but less helpful in determining underlying causes. The exam is focused primarily on the genital area. For example, a palpable plaque may be found that signifies an underlying problem with Peyronie's disease. Finding of small, soft testes or even breast tissue enlargement (gynecomastia) alerts one to a further endocrine evaluation. This type of patient may have a low testosterone level or even a prolactin-secreting benign tumor (Prolactinoma). Patients with certain genetic syndromes, such as Kallmann's or Klinefelter's syndrome, have obvious physical signs of not only small, poorly-developed testicles, but a distinctive overall body appearance.

In patients with known diabetes, a careful neurological exam is important. A peripheral neuropathy may be established in these patients or others having not yet been diagnosed with diabetes. Evaluating genital and pelvic sensation is also useful in assessing the role of a possible neurological etiology. Vascular status can be assessed with the evaluation of the pulses in both lower extremities along with the temperature of the lower extremities, as well as the temperature of the penis. For example, if one leg is significantly colder than the other, this certainly suggests some peripheral vascular occlusive disease that would deserve further evaluation. The rectal exam is also important. Evidence of benign or malignant prostate disease is easily obtained from the digital rectal exam.

In a recent study,[57] patients with erectile dysfunction were carefully evaluated by history, physical exam, psychological evaluation and nighttime penile tumescence monitoring (using the Rigiscan) and additional lab testing. In this study, the history and physical examination have a 95 percent sensitivity with only a 50 percent specificity in diagnosing organic erectile dysfunction. There is no doubt that a multi-factorial approach is required to fully evaluate patients with erectile dysfunction. On the other hand, from a practical standpoint, a very careful history and physical exam today will direct the physician to the most cost-effective and expedient form of management, and obviate the need for unnecessary, costly diagnostic testes.

Now that Viagra is available as a safe oral medication, the most important part of the history is the category under "current medication." As long as the patient has no history of use of nitroglycerine and other nitrates, he is potentially a very good candidate to try Viagra as the first line of therapy. In considering which lab studies to obtain next, with the availability of Viagra, this is now limited to a urinalysis to make sure the patient has no evidence of occult diabetes, renal disease, or urinary tract infection. If the patient's history reveals a significant amount of decrease in libido, or if the physical exam reveals a lot of atrophy and loss of normal size and volume of each testicle, a blood testosterone level is certainly indicated. Those patients with low serum testosterone, for example, will definitely benefit on a long-term basis from testosterone replacement [See Chapter 6], even if the Viagra solves their erectile dysfunction problem. A blood prolactin level need not be done on patients routinely, unless the testosterone level is quite low. In those patients with a low testosterone level, a repeat test along with evaluation of other pituitary gland hormones (Lutenizing hormone, follicle stimulating hormone, and prolactin) is indicated. While erectile dysfunction may not be directly affected by low testosterone levels, the effects of a diminished sex drive, based on a low testosterone, may contribute to the erectile dysfunction problem.

In this era, with the availability of Viagra, with its tremendously successful track record in treating male erectile dysfunction problems, no further tests are usually indicated at this point. When patients come back to see us in the office who have tried Viagra and have not had success or when individuals are initially seen, who have known coronary artery disease, with a history of significant obstruction to blood vessels in the heart causing a need for nitrate-type medicines, therefore preventing their use of Viagra, the next step in evaluation and management is also very straightforward. I refer to this as the Pre-Viagra Treatment Protocol. After consultation with the patient and his partner, there are four areas of nonsurgical treatment to offer the patient. While surgical treatment with a penile implant has a high success rate (95 percent), most patients prefer a trial of one or more of the nonsurgical approaches before making the decision for surgery [see Chapter 11].

The first includes an empirical injection of the male hormone testosterone [see Chapter 6], which would be expected to provide some benefit to libido, and in some patients actually improves their erectile function. The second choice would be one of several available vasoactive drugs. The injection of these drugs directly into the erectile tissue of the penis a few minutes prior to intercourse has the greatest chance of successfully resulting in an adequate erection [See Chapter 7]. However, when given the choice of an injection using a needle versus a urethral suppository introduced into the tip of the penis [see Chapter 9], most patients initially will opt for the urethral suppository. Unfortunately, the success rate with the urethral suppository is less than 30 percent versus greater than 90 percent overall success with the penile injections. In those patients in whom the urethral suppository is not effective or causes painful side effects, or where the patient "doesn't want a needle," another option is the use of a vacuum erection device [See Chapter 10].

An injection of one of the vasoactive drugs into one of the erectile cylinders of the penis can be both diagnostic and therapeutic. In those patients in the office that have an excellent response to a small dose of one of the vasoactive drugs, we know that they have good circulation to the penis, and that the etiology of their problem may be either neurologic or psychological. Those patients then have the option of using this injection procedure for management for their erectile dysfunction problem [see Chapter 7 for more details]. On the other hand, those individuals who do not respond in the office to injection with vasoactive drugs are usually suffering with significant vascular occlusive disease. Once it's determined that they are not going to respond to the injection protocol, they may want to try one of the vacuum erection devices or proceed with one of the more complex vascular evaluations. Those individuals may be candidates for vascular surgery or certainly may simply desire a more accurate assessment of their arterial function [See Chapter 11]. At this point in the evaluation and the management of a patient with erectile dysfunction, it's important to educate the patient regarding possible lifestyle modifications that may be of benefit. These include a better diet to lower the cholesterol levels, along with more exercise, stress reduction, and a discussion of the role of alcohol and smoking. These changes in lifestyle, while difficult to correlate with any beneficial effect, however, certainly improve the patient's overall health status. Lue and associates [58,59] have used a patient's goal-directed approach in determining the extent of the workup, given that the actual goal of the patient and his partner will vary according to the patient's age, his overall general health, and his treatment goals.

Nocturnal Penile Tumescence (NPT) Testing

Nocturnal penile tumescence, the sleep-related erection, occurs in virtually all potent men. In 1965, studies first revealed the association of the nocturnal penile erection with the REM phase.[62] In 1970 Dr. I. Karacan[63] suggested the NPT could be used to evaluate male erectile dysfunction, assuming that the mechanism of the nighttime erection relied on the same type of neurovascular responses similar to the awake erotically-induced erections. Thus, patients with documented normal NPT are presumed to have a normal capacity for a spontaneous, erotically-induced erection. The primary goal of NPT testing is to distinguish psychological causes from physical (organic) causes or impotence. In the 1970s, the penile prosthesis was developed for treatment of patients with significant erectile dysfunction. Before undergoing surgery, it was important to be certain the patient had a physical problem and not a psychological problem. At that time, sleep labs were established. While this provided a lot of useful information, these studies were quite costly, requiring at least three nights of stay in the sleep lab. This gave rise to two other more simplified means of assessing nighttime penile tumescence. The first method involved simply the use of a ring of postage stamps. This was called a stamp test, and was popularized in the early eighties in the ambulatory urology office setting.[64, 65] This technique involved having the patient simply place a ring of postage stamps around the penis at night and check the next morning to see if he had enough tumescence while asleep to break the ring. This test is only qualitative, in that it does not tell how many erections or to what rigidity had been obtained during nighttime tumescence. To make the postage stamp test more accurate, a new snap-gauge device was developed. This consists of a combination of three narrow, plastic tapes designed to rupture at different forces, mounted on a Velcro fastener that snaps around the penis. A narrow blue strip, fitting rather snugly, is designed to rupture with 10 ounces of pressure. A narrow red tape is set to rupture at 15 ounces, and a clear tape, which fits the most loosely, is set to snap at about 20 ounces of pressure. Either the postage stamp or the snap-gauge test has to be done over two or three nights to make sure the patient has at least one or more episodes of REM sleep to adequately test the nighttime erection.

Patients occasionally come back to the office and report that they didn't break the snap-gauge at all; however, they didn't try the test until the night before their second office visit, and they were up half the night drinking coffee and were anxious about the test and probably didn't have any REM sleep cycles at all. In patients with normal nighttime erections, often the snapping of the snap-gauge bands will make a loud popping noise and awaken the patient. Even though the snap-gauge test is very economical, its accuracy in distinguishing physical erectile dysfunction from psychological erectile dysfunction has been questioned.[66-69]

Ultimately, concerns over the accuracy of rigidity monitoring and the cost of sleep laboratory evaluation led to the development of Rigiscan, a small, portable monitoring system, which continuously measures the rigidity of the erect penis as well as records the number and duration of each tumescent episode. This device combines complicated monitoring with the convenience and economic advantage of an ambulatory monitoring system.[70] While the Rigiscan monitor certainly provides a lot more information about numbers of erections and duration of each erection, along with degree of rigidity, there have been objections from physiologists who feel the lack of accurate sleep stage simultaneous information may lead to some misinterpretation.

Sleep Lab Studies

As mentioned earlier, the advent of sleep lab studies in the 1970s provided the urologists who were doing penile implant surgery with very important information. At that time, for a large number of patients the choice of treatment was between psychological counseling and penile implant surgery. Thus, sleep lab data was used more to rule out a primary psychological problem, preventing an unnecessary surgical procedure on someone who might benefit from a course of psychological counseling. The sleep laboratory NPT testing today is used in only selected cases. For example, it's helpful in patients who have very confusing histories, and those involved in litigation where compensation may be based on the cause of the patient's erectile status problem. In cases where Rigiscan data is not conclusive, a sleep lab study can rule out sleep apnea and other sleep disorders, as well as confirm the Rigiscan data.[71]

Other Tests

Three additional tests are available to study the vascular supply to the erectile cylinders. Duplex ultrasound is useful when patients may have erectile dysfunction caused by problems with arterial blood flow. This study could also provide helpful information regarding venous-occlusive dysfunction. The standard diagnostic study for veno-occlusive dysfunction is pharmacologic cavernosometry and cavernosography.

Cavernosometry involves infusing saline into the corpus cavernosum — the erectile cylinders — while monitoring the intracorporal pressure. This can be done with or without the intracavernous injection of a vasodilating agent such as papaverine or alprostadil.

The cavernosography study involves the infusion of X-ray contrast solution instead of just normal saline into the corpora cavernosa during an artificial erection created by the introduction of a vasodilating drug. This technique helps demonstrate the site of a venous leakage.

These last three studies are not to be done by primary care physicians or even most urologists in their office during the first and second stages of evaluation of the patient with erectile dysfunction. These studies should be done only in referral centers where large numbers of patients are evaluated daily. The vast majority of patients with erectile dysfunction may be evaluated and treated successfully and never undergo any of these three studies.

Plain Talk Summary of Evaluating Erectile Dysfunction

The evaluation of the male with erectile dysfunction consists of four components: the medical history, the psychosexual history, the physical examination, and selected laboratory and diagnostic tests.

The medical history provides insight into conditions that may be contributing to the problem. During the medical history we want to identify risk factors that will help us determine whether the patient's problem is physical rather than psychological. In addition, a few medical conditions will allow medical treatment based on the history. For example, if the patient is on certain antihypertensive medications that may be changed to other drugs that would cause fewer side effects, this would be an important discovery. A history of certain previous operations, such as radical prostate surgery or rectal surgery, indicates that a patient's problem is likely physical in nature. A history of risk factors for vascular disease and risk factors for impotence, such as cigarette smoking or a history of elevated blood cholesterol levels, also helps in determining that the patient's problem is primarily physical rather than primarily psychological. A history of curvature of the penis, suggestive of Peyronie's disease, a history of alcohol or drug abuse, or a history of significant vascular disease involving coronary arteries or arteries to the lower extremities or carotid arteries helps establish a systemic problem with vascular-occlusive disease.

The psychosexual history is by far the most important part of the history in determining the course of therapy. Now that Viagra is available as a safe, oral agent that works in a broad spectrum of patients with various physical causes, our main purpose in the psychosexual history is to identify those individuals whose erectile dysfunction has a primarily psychological cause. Regardless of how successfully we as urologists or primary care physicians can restore a male patient's erection, if the relationship with his partner is in terrible shape, the couple will still have a very unsatisfactory sex life. Most patients who come into a urologist's office with erectile dysfunction complaints are over the age of 40 and are stable individuals with the same sexual partner for over 20 years, with good support from their wife or sexual partner. Knowing the history of problems with libido or sex drive is very important. Decreased libido may be either primary, due to a decrease in the level of testosterone, or secondary to the erectile dysfunction itself, with the patient preferring to avoid the "fear of failure." Patients with significantly depressed libido will need examination of their blood testosterone level. Meanwhile, in those individuals with a normal libido, the blood testosterone level would be of little value. Ejaculation dysfunction along with erectile dysfunction often is seen in patients with primarily a psychological etiology. Questions regarding the early morning erections, that are present in all potent men, are helpful also in distinguishing psychological and physical problems. Those individuals with physical contributory factors to their erectile dysfunction usually will have a diminished, if not absent, early morning erection. Those individuals with a primarily psychological cause to their erectile dysfunction will usually be quick to say they still have early morning erections most of the time.

The physical examination specifically looks for signs of vascular insufficiency. A focused neurological exam with evaluation of the sensation of the penis and the evaluation of the erectile sphincter tone, as well as the size and consistency of the prostate gland, is important. Examination of the penis may yield a finding of Peyronie's disease with plaque formation. Examination of secondary male sexual characteristics, such as testicular size and volume, and the presence and amount of facial hair and genital hair is also helpful.

Laboratory tests should include a urinalysis. A blood testosterone level is indicated if the patient is complaining of a significant decrease in libido, or if there is an insufficiency in the normal secondary sexual characteristics. Most patients with erectile dysfunction do not require an extensive or complicated series of tests before they can receive effective treatment. For example, occasionally a patient has an excess of serum blood prolactin that causes a decrease in libido and a decreased blood testosterone level. Every patient does not need a blood prolactin level test. This should be reserved only for the individuals with a marked decrease in testosterone. At this point in the evaluation process, before the availability of Viagra in April of 1998, the overall objective goals of the patient and his partner were discussed. If they wanted only a minimal noninvasive therapeutic approach, an empirical injection of the male hormone, Depo-Testosterone, or a trial of an oral agent, such as Yohimbine, were frequently recommended. The success rate on those two empirical treatments was quite low. Once the vasoactive drugs gained popularity in the early 1980s, the urologists evaluating a patient with erectile dysfunction could quickly move to the test injection of a vasoactive drug into the erectile tissue. This was both diagnostic and clinically important. Patients who did respond to one of several vasoactive injections in the office had the option of using this protocol at home. Patients who did not respond were felt to have a significant compromise to the vascular supply to the erectile tissue and, in all likelihood, would probably require a penile implant, with or without any additional extensive vascular testing.

Today, with the availability of Viagra, the first step after the history and physical exam is to start the patient on Viagra. After a four- to six-week trial with Viagra, if the patient is not having a successful response, we continue the assessment with the "Pre-Viagra" protocol. Even when Viagra is not successful, most urologists will have the patient evaluated, and on a treatment protocol within two additional office visits.

In those patients whose erectile dysfunction is not solved by Viagra, nocturnal penile tumescence (NPT) testing may further help differentiate psychological dysfunction from physical dysfunction. This test can be performed by several methods, including a simple snap-gauge test, the Rigiscan device, or a more formal sleep laboratory. The latter two techniques are reserved for those patients who have a high likelihood of having a psychological problem, or those in whom some type of financial settlement or litigation depends on an accurate assessment of the cause of their erectile dysfunction.

For those very few patients who have a primary vascular problem that is surgically correctable [see Chapter 10], there are more complicated tests available, including Duplex ultrasound studies and dynamic infusion cavernosography and cavernosometry (DICC). These more invasive studies are generally reserved for those very rare patients who will require vascular surgery or consideration of vascular surgery.

5

METABOLIC DISORDERS

Treatment Strategies
for Diabetes, Prolactinoma

Diabetes is the number one single cause of male erectile dysfunction, accounting for about 40 percent of all impotence cases.[72, 73] Other endocrine, or hormonal, causes are far less common,[74] accounting for only about 4 percent of all cases of male erectile dysfunction. However, when these few other cases are properly recognized and properly treated, the result is often a marked improvement without any further treatment. Endocrine disorders can be grouped into three general categories: diabetes mellitus, elevated prolactin levels (hyperprolactinemia), and a third group including a number of chronic disorders, most of which suppress testosterone, thereby resulting in decreased libido with secondary erectile dysfunction [see Table 2].

Diabetes Mellitus

Diabetes mellitus is a disease of metabolic deregulation, specifically of glucose metabolism. In other words, the body's ability to process sugar-type compounds in food breaks down. Diabetes is accompanied by several characteristic longterm complications and side effects. Two types of patients have diabetes. The first are categorized as Type I, or insulin-dependent diabetics. Type II patients are non-insulin-dependent. Both types suffer from the side effects of small-vessel disease, causing retinal damage and renal problems affecting overall kidney function. Both groups are also susceptible to larger-vessel occlusive disease affecting coronary arteries in the heart and the cerebrovascular vessels supplying the brain. Both groups are also susceptible to peripheral nerve damage (peripheral neuropathy).

Erectile dysfunction in most diabetics is due to chronic complications involving both the small-vessel disease and the nerve damage/neuropathy. From 35 to 70 percent of diabetic patients will develop erectile dysfunction as a complication of the disease. When seeing diabetic patients who have peripheral nerve damage problem and subsequent complaints — for example, lower extremity numbness or burning in the lower extremities — we can predict that most of them will already have erectile dysfunction.

However, there are always exceptions, and it is certainly not impossible for a diabetic individual to have primarily psychological problems as the cause of erectile dysfunction. Again, the importance of a very thorough history and psychosexual history cannot be overemphasized. The added stress of erectile dysfunction, particularly in diabetic men under age 40, increases anxiety and depression. This often makes separation of these two potential causes a bit more difficult.[75]

Thus, while we can expect diabetics to develop erectile dysfunction, its progression can be very slow, from months to years. Once the symptom of erectile dysfunction has been observed, the best way to prevent it from progressing is to maintain strict blood sugar control.[76] Diabetic patients with progressive erectile dysfunction should be treated like nondiabetic patients with erectile dysfunction. Other forms of treatment, including oral Viagra, pharmacologic agents that are injected or placed in the urethra with the suppository or penile implants are discussed in upcoming chapters.

Prolactinoma

Prolactin is a hormone that contributes to milk production in lactating females. In males, prolactin at normal levels basically does nothing. But at excessive levels (hyperprolactinemia), it decreases sex

Table 2: Conditions of Erectile Dysfunction Associated with Hormonal Disorders

Congenital developmental disorders of androgen deficiency (birth defects that cause low testosterone)
    Hypergonadotropic hypogonadism
        Klinefelter's syndrome (for example)
        Other rare conditions
    Hypogonadotropic hypogonadism
        Kallmann's syndrome (for example)
        Other rare conditions
    17-Ketosteroid reductase deficiency
    Androgen resistance syndromes
        Reifenstein's syndrome

Men aging normally

Acquired gonadal failure

Systemic disorders
        Chronic liver disease
        Autoimmune deficiency syndrome (AIDS)
        Chronic renal failure
        Sickle cell disease
        Nutritional disorders
        Medication effects

Specific endocrine disorders
        Hypothalamic-pituitary
        Nonfunctioning tumors
        Functioning pituitary tumors
        Prolactinomas
        Other benign lesions

Hyperprolactinemia thyroid disorders

Adrenal disorders

Diabetes Mellitus

drive and leads to erectile dysfunction. In the earlier section on patient evaluation, we emphasized the importance of looking for a low serum testosterone level before ordering a test for prolactin level.

When the prolactin level is elevated, a large number of problems, conditions, and medications can be responsible, including the benign pituitary tumor, prolactinoma [See Table 3]. Patients with a significant elevation of the serum prolactin are best referred to the endocrinologist for management. These specialists will evaluate the patient further to rule out medications that might be causing the elevated prolactin, and will do studies to distinguish between idiopathic hyperprolactinemia and pro-lactin-secreting tumors, or prolactinomas. Idiopathic hyperprolactinemia can be managed with drugs only, whereas prolactinomas sometimes require surgery and radiation. However, medical therapy is highly effective using Bromocriptine. Once Bromocriptine treatment is started, the time to tumor reduction and return of testosterone to normal levels varies according to the size of the tumor. Sometimes, the return to a normal testosterone level is delayed for up to six to twelve months.[77] Newer oral medication for prolactin-secreting pituitary tumors is on the horizon.

Plain Talk Summary of Correction of Metabolic Disorders

Metabolic disorders contributing to erectile dysfunction may be grouped into one of three categories. These include diabetes mellitus, conditions leading to elevated blood levels of the pituitary gland hor-mone, prolactin (hyperprolactinemia), and conditions that contribute to a low level of the male hormone, testosterone. The next chapter will focus on the treatment options for hormone replacement.

As we have stated on several occasions in this text, diabetes mellitus is the single most common disorder that causes erectile dysfunction. It does so by affecting both the neurologic and vascular mechanism that lead to a normal erection. Up to 50 percent of patients with diabetes may expect to have a problem with erectile dysfunction in their lifetime. As is the case with other side effects from diabetes, erectile dysfunction is best managed by early diagnosis and subsequent tight control of blood sugars.

Diabetic patients may first present to the primary care physician or urologist complaining of erectile dysfunction as their first and most noticeable symptom. Diabetic patients frequently have normal libido and usually have a lot of performance anxiety caused by the erectile dysfunction problem. It's important also to remember that just because a patient, who also happens to be diabetic, is complaining of erectile dysfunction, we as clinicians can't simply assume the erectile dysfunction is a complication of the diabetes. All diabetic patients deserve a very thorough psychosexual history, and often NPT testing should be used to help establish that the patient's problem is primarily physical versus psychological.

Hyperprolactinemia (elevated blood levels of prolactin) is another common endocrine cause of erectile dysfunction. Elevated prolactin causes both a significant decrease in libido, as well as a decrease in serum testosterone levels. Serum prolactin levels need not be measured in every patient with erectile dysfunction, but it certainly should in those with decreased libido. Men with significantly depressed serum testosterone levels should have a serum prolactin measurement. It's important to understand that a large number of chronic illnesses and medications can contribute to elevated blood prolactin levels. All patients with an elevated prolactin level should be referred to an endocrinologist, who will further evaluate the patient to establish the presence or absence of a prolactin-secreting, benign tumor in the pituitary gland. At present, there are oral medications available for control of the prolactin level. Sometimes it does take several months to see a return of the prolactin level to normal and a return of the testosterone level back up to normal levels, as well.

Table 3: Causes of Hyperprolactinemia

Pituitary tumor
  Other rare benign lesions
Hypothalamic disease
  Craniopharyngioma
  Meningiomas
  Other rare benign problmes
Neurogenic/traumatic
  Chest wall surgery or trauma
  Spinal cord lesions
Medications
  Dopamine receptor antagonists (phenothiazine)
  Monoamine inhibitors (alfa-methyldopa)
  Monoamine depleters (reserpine)
  Metoclopramide
  Amoxepin
  Verapamil
  Cocaine
Other
  Primary hypothyroidism
  Renal failure
  Cirrhosis

6

THE TESTOSTERONE EFFECT

Hormone Replacement Therapy

Testosterone replacement is currently used today in both primary and secondary hypogonadism (decreased testicular production of testosterone). The current methods of androgen replacement available for human use include oral preparations (17 alpha-alkylated derivatives), the injectable long-acting esters of testosterone (enanthate and cypionate), and the transdermal preparations (Testoderm and Androderm).

The oral androgen preparations, the methyl testosterone products, have been available since the 1970s and have been popular. They were popular at a time before we had injections with vasoactive drugs or vacuum erection devices, and before penile implants became more widely used. Unfortunately, these preparations have the potential for serious liver damage. For patients who cannot take the injectable form of testosterone, or cannot use the patches, the oral methyl testosterone at doses of 25 to 50 mg. per day may be used as long as there is close monitoring of liver function.

The esterified testosterone products, Depo-Testosterone, and testosterone enanthate, are given with intramuscular injections at doses of 200 to 400 mg. every three to four weeks. This form of testosterone replacement has been popular for the last 30 years. It has the obvious disadvantage of peaks and valleys in blood levels of testosterone. It is therefore far from an ideal physiologic replacement. On the other hand, in patients with low serum testosterone levels who also have erectile dysfunction, the evaluation of the effects of an injection of Depo-Testosterone takes only a few days.

The transdermal preparations, Testoderm and Androderm, are more convenient. An office visit for an injection is not required. They are more reliable in maintaining a more natural testosterone level and more closely mimic the normal physiologic testosterone secretion.[78, 79] With a transdermal patch normal serum testosterone levels can be achieved in more than 90 percent of patients. The most common adverse events described have been itching (7 percent), chronic skin irritation (2 to 5 percent), and allergic dermatitis (4 percent). With the patches the peak level of testosterone occurs between two and six hours after the patch application, followed by a gradual decrease in the next 24 hours; therefore, the patches have to be applied daily.

Exactly how low serum testosterone contributes to erectile dysfunction is still unclear. It may be more of a central mechanism affecting libido than affecting penile tissue itself. However, a recent report[80] suggests there may be a direct effect of testosterone on the erectile tissue. From a clinical standpoint, however, the effectiveness of hormone replacement in men with low testosterone levels has been rather disappointing. A recent clinical study[81] involving men with low testosterone levels, reported only a 9 percent response rate for patients treated with oral androgen replacement. In some young males with insufficient testosterone, hormone replacement has a greater chance of resulting in a modest improvement in erectile function.[12] The majority of older men usually suffer from a combination of neurovascular problems that outweigh the singular effects of testosterone deficiency on erectile dysfunction. Therefore, while it's important for such patients to maintain reasonably normal levels of blood testosterone for other clinical reasons, such as bone metabolism, they are less likely to see a profound response in their erectile function.

Testosterone therapy is contraindicated in men with prostate cancer. It is relatively contraindicated in older men with bladder neck obstruction from prostate enlargement. It is recommended that all men over the age of 50 receiving androgen, testosterone, initially have a prostate specific antigen level measurement along with a digital rectal exam. When patients take androgen replacement therapy, the outside source of testosterone can suppress production of testosterone by the testicles, leading to testicular atrophy. The extra testosterone may also be converted to estradiol, an estrogen substance, that potentially may be detrimental to sexual function.

Plain Talk Summary of Hormonal Replacement Therapy

While hormone replacement therapy is easy to administer, reasonably safe, and reasonably inexpensive, it is not without increased risks and side effects. All males over the age of 50 who are treated with extra testosterone, whether by injections or skin patches, should be aware of the potential side effects, including aggravation of any occult (present, but causing symptoms) cancer of the prostate. All males over the age of 50 should have an annual digital rectal examination along with a blood PSA level, as a minimum. In addition, oral testosterone preparations definitely increase the risk of liver problems, requiring close monitoring of liver function in those few individuals who are best managed with the oral methyltestosterone preparations. Although all of us who treat patients with erectile dysfunction have a number of patients in our practice who swear by the positive effects of their monthly Depo-Testosterone injection, control studies have revealed less than a 10 percent improvement rate for men with erectile dysfunction. In those patients with a severely depressed serum testosterone level, consultation with an endocrinologist is advised before initiating any hormone replacement therapy with any of the testosterone preparations.

7

GIVE IT A SHOT

Penile Injections With Vasoactive Drugs

While the development of the penile prosthesis technology was the breakthrough treatment of the 1970s for treating erectile dysfunction, the exciting contribution of the early 1980s was when the French researcher Virag first reported his finding of erections induced by injecting papaverine into the penis.[82] The intracavernous injection technique exploded across America after that. At the national urology meeting in 1983 one urologist personally demonstrated the effects of an intracorporous injection by doing a self-injection a few minutes before his lecture. He then walked out into the audience so those in attendance could have an up close and personal appreciation of the effects of his intracavernous injection. This was undoubtedly the first "hands on" demonstration in the U.S. for intracavernous injection therapy.

The penile injection protocols that followed have been a major contribution to the treatment of male erectile dysfunction for almost two decades now. The experience in the mid-1980s was primarily with papaverine alone. Later papaverine was used in combination with phentolamine (Regitine). Prostaglandin E_1 (PGE_1) became available toward the end of the 1980s along with the synthetic form, alprostadil. More recently, over the last seven years, a combination of papaverine, phentolamine, and PGE_1 (Tri-Mix) has been utilized. While other medications have been utilized in clinical trials, these three preparations have received the most use and are now prescribed worldwide. Literally millions of couples around the world have been able to experience satisfying sexual intercourse as a result of treatment with injection of these vasoactive drugs.

The process itself is quite simple. Injection of 0.1 cc up to 1.0 cc of one of the drugs into either the right or left corpus cavernosum near the base of the penis, followed by a gentle squeezing of that area, circulates the drug to both erectile cylinders, resulting in an erection in 10 to 15 minutes [See Figure 6].

Papaverine

Papaverine is derived from the opium poppy. Its molecular action is related to its inhibitory effect on phosphodiesterase, leading to increased levels of cAMP and cGMP in penile erectile tissue, its blockage of calcium channels, and a subsequent increase in calcium eflux from cells. All of these actions promote smooth muscle relaxation in the penile arteries and sinusoids. In plain talk, papaverine stimulates the engorgement of the penis with blood, leading to a harder erection.

Papaverine has a very high success rate, particularly in younger patients who have better erectile potential to begin with, and in patients whose erectile dysfunction is primarily psychological or nerve-related. The primary advantages of papaverine are its low cost and its stability at room temperature.

Various studies have reported papaverine alone to result in a full erection in 35 to 60 percent of the males studied.[83-85]

In the office setting, I let the patient do the very first injection under watchful supervision. He injects 0.1 cc (3 mg.) on his initial monitored injection in the office. Sometimes that dose gives a satisfactory erection. Once the patient is checked out on the injection procedure, he is allowed to gradually increase the dose at home. This obviates the need for multiple and expensive recurrent office visits. The two major disadvantages are a rather variable incidence of priapism, where the penis stays erect for many hours, and corporal fibrosis (buildup of scar tissue).

Fibrosis occurs as a result of the injection itself, from irritation of the cells when penetrated by the needle and as the fluid is injected, and occasionally by damage to the penile tissue as a result of priapism. Up to 20 percent incidence of corporal fibrosis has been reported. In order to reduce that incidence, patients are instructed to inject no more than every third night and to suspend injections if they notice scarring in the erectile cylinders. Scarring can also be minimized by alternating the sides of the penis where the injection is given.

Priapism risk is small, but can be further reduced by starting the patient with a very low dose of papaverine. When a sustained erection does occur, it is because the drug has dilated the blood vessels, allowing engorgement and an erection, but then after orgasm the vessels do not constrict as they would with a natural erection. Thus, the penis can remain hard, sometimes for hours and hours. We instruct patients to keep some type of alpha adrenergic, such as Sudafed, on hand at home to counteract this side effect. If taking Sudafed does not cause a return to the flaccid state, the patient has to come to the emergency room where the urologist irrigates the erectile cylinders with a very dilute epinephrine solution. This helps constrict blood vessels, and prevents their sustained dilation and prevents the persistent erection. Priapism induced by intracorporal injections can usually be treated promptly and successfully by the urologist in the emergency room.

However, a prolonged erection (24-36 hours) can produce more intracorporal fibrosis, and additional problems of erectile dysfunction. Primary care physicians are not trained in handling this complication — it occurs in less than 2 percent of patients — and ordinarily should not be managing patients with intracorporal injections.

On rare occasions patients experience systemic side effects from papaverine intracorporal injections, including dizziness, diaphoresis and cold sweats, which may be the result of either a vaso-vegal reflex or hypotension from the vasodilatory effect in patients with veno-occlusive dysfunction. One recent study reported systemic papaverine levels after intracavernous injection. The researchers in this study found a significantly higher peripheral blood level in those patients with poor erectile

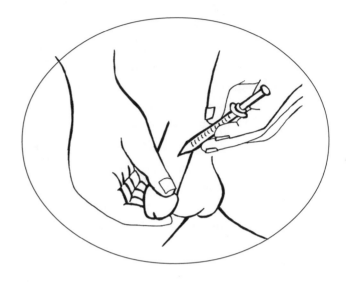

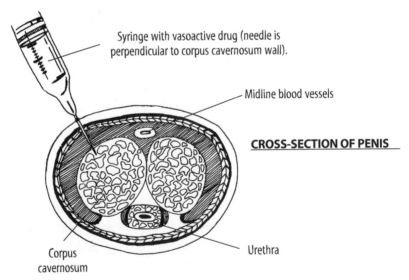

Syringe with vasoactive drug (needle is perpendicular to corpus cavernosum wall).

Midline blood vessels

CROSS-SECTION OF PENIS

Corpus cavernosum

Urethra

Fig. 6: Injection of Vasoactive Drug into Penis

response, suggestive of veno-occlusive dysfunction.

Incidentally, the question may come up that papaverine is not Food and Drug Administration (FDA) approved for injecting into the penis. This does not mean the drug is not safe. In fact, it is so safe that up until Viagra it was probably the most widely used drug in treating erectile dysfunction. But the erection-inducing effects of papaverine were discovered somewhat accidentally. The drug had been in use already, and had been FDA approved, for other medical procedures involving vascular dilation. Then, the effects on erectile dysfunction were so profound and became widespread so quickly that the drug was already in common usage for penile injections before an FDA study could have been organized. Doctors already knew the drug was safe; this was simply a new application. And retrospective studies have confirmed its safety for penile injections. But the drug is so safe and so inexpensive that the company making it never felt it was necessary to pay for a full-scale FDA approval process.

Papaverine — Phentolamine Combination

The drug phentolamine (Regitine) alone has been found to be ineffective in producing an erection.[84] But in 1985, it was first reported that a combination of papaverine with phentolamine had an overall effectiveness rate of 72 percent.[86] The incidence of prolonged erection, priapism, was less than 2 percent during those early studies, while fibrosis of the erectile cylinders developed in less than 5 percent. Since more studies have been reported, the incidence of priapism has ranged from as low as 1 percent up to 23 percent, while fibrosis has ranged from 2 percent up to 16 percent.[87, 88] This combination seems to be equally effective with patients over 65, compared with a group of men 20 years younger.[88] With the addition of phentolamine (Regitine) to papaverine, we now are up to greater than 70 percent success in helping patients achieve an erection. The largest negative with the addition of phentolamine has been the cost. Whereas, a 10 cc bottle of papaverine can be purchased for less than $20, the addition of Regitine increases the cost fourfold, up to $80 to $90 a bottle. This translates into a cost increase from $1 per injection for papaverine alone versus $5 per injection for the combination of papaverine plus Regitine. The benefit, of course, is the reduction of unwanted side effects that may occur more often than with papaverine alone.

Prostaglandin E₁ (Alprostadil)

Alprostadil is the synthetic form of a naturally occurring unsaturated fatty acid that causes smooth muscle relaxation and vasodilation. It had been used for peripheral vascular disease long before being applied to penile injection therapy. The drug is almost totally metabolized within the intracavernous tissue.[89] No change in peripheral blood levels has been observed.[90] In most patients with veno-occlusive dysfunction the alprostadil level may rise to ten times baseline, but up to 90 percent of the drug is metabolized on the first pass through the lungs. This minimizes the incidence of prolonged systemic side effects.

Several formulations of alprostadil have been produced. Caverject, a freeze-dried (lyophilized) powder, was specifically developed for intracavernous injection. Since its first report of being safe and effective for home injection therapy in 1988, it has gained a wide acceptance.[91] Caverject was the first drug approved by the FDA for treating erectile dysfunction. Several studies indicated that it was slightly more effective than papaverine alone, but about the same level of effectiveness as the combination of papaverine plus Regitine. Up to 80 percent of patients, unfortunately, have pain at the injection site or during erection, while less than 2 percent had problems with prolonged erection and priapism. Another major disadvantage to Caverject has been its cost. Depending on the dose required, the patient may easily be spending $40 to $50 per injection. This is 50 times more expensive than papaverine alone. Thus, while Caverject has been shown to be highly effective in large scale studies,[92, 93] other studies were carried out, looking at other combinations of drugs to help reduce the cost and decrease the painful injection.

Papaverine — Phentolamine — Alprostadil

In 1991, Bennett, et al., introduced a three-drug mixture containing papaverine, phentolamine, and alprostadil for intracavernous injection.[94] Each of these drugs has a different mechanism. Theoretically, in combination a smaller dose of each would be effective, thus avoiding the side effects of higher dosages. In this study, 89 percent of the patients had a satisfactory erection and went on to the self-injection protocol at home. With longer follow-up, up to 28 months, 65 percent of this group continued to use this injection therapy with an 89 percent satisfaction rate. No reports of fibrosis were recorded and the prolonged erection incidence was about 5 percent. In summary, this triple drug combination, known as Tri-Mix, has been shown to be as effective as alprostadil alone, with a somewhat lower incidence of painful erections.

Patient Acceptance

The patient acceptance rate of penile injections varies from 50 to 85 percent. Some patients just don't want to use the needle or have an inadequate response to the test dose in the office. Over the long term, 15 to 60 percent of patients drop out for a number of reasons including loss of interest, loss of partner, poor erectile response, penile pain, recovery of spontaneous erection, or ultimately choosing some other type of therapy.

The use of intracavernous injection therapy is not recommended in patients with sickle cell anemia, schizophrenia, severe psychiatric disorders, severe venous incompetence, or severe systemic disease. Patients who take an anticoagulant or aspirin should compress the injection site for ten minutes after injection. For patients with poor manual dexterity or motor control, the sexual partner can be instructed in the injection technique.

Recovery of Spontaneous Erections

One of the reasons I encourage patients with significant erectile dysfunction to try intracorporal injection, with any of the above drugs, is that a certain percentage of patients will see a significant improvement in their spontaneous erections and ultimately may not have to use the injection protocol at all. From reports in the literature,[95, 96] patients with a psychological cause to their erectile dysfunction have as high as a 90 percent chance of return to natural spontaneous erections. Those patients with physical causes may see a complete recovery of normal spontaneous erections from 10 to 15 percent of the time and a partial recovery up to 65 percent of the time. Some patients in the group with the partial recovery continue to inject about one-half to one-third of the time, but in between they can have spontaneous erections. It's always gratifying to hear a patient tell me that he keeps "the papaverine in the medicine cabinet at home as a backup, but most of the time I don't need it." In general, those patients whose penile blood flow is closer to normal will get a good response to a small dose of papaverine and are more likely to be able to gradually discontinue injections and return to satisfactory, spontaneous erections. On the other hand, individuals who require larger doses of a mixture of papaverine plus Regitine generally have a more significant underlying physical problem and are less likely to be able to leave off the papaverine and Regitine mixture completely.

Plain Talk Summary of Injections With Vasoactive Drugs

Since the early 1980s, intracavernous injection therapy has played a major role in treating patients with both psychological and physical impotence. Injection of intracavernous drugs in the office setting can be both diagnostic and subsequently therapeutic. There are currently four different regimens available for injection: papaverine, papaverine plus phentolamine, prostaglandin E_1 (alprostadil), and a combination of papaverine, phentolamine, and alprostadil (the synthetic prostaglandin E_1). Each of these agents has its advantages and disadvantages, which were summarized in this chapter. While injection therapy is not first line therapy, now with the availability of Viagra as an oral agent, injection therapy has moved from second line to third line therapy. Even with the side effects of penile fibrosis, sustained erection (priapism), and penile pain, the benefits of this injection technique, with any of the above agents for the last 15 years has been tremendous. The injection protocol has returned many men to normal function and preserved many marriages.

With the availability of Viagra as the now accepted first line of therapy, the second line of therapy includes less invasive procedures involving intraurethral suppositories and vacuum erection devices, which will be discussed in the upcoming chapters.

8

The MUSE of Erections

Urethral Suppository
with Vasoactive Drugs

In early 1997 the intraurethral administration of alprostadil became available for clinical use after being approved by the FDA. The dose is introduced through a small, plastic applicator placed inside the opening of the urethra [See Figure 7]. The doses delivered by the intraurethral administrations, however, are significantly larger (usually 500 to 1000 micrograms) than the dose delivered by intracavernous injection. In the largest study on this route of introduction of alprostadil,[95] approximately two-thirds of the patients tested in the office setting had a subsequent erection adequate for intercourse. In this report, 50 percent achieved successful intercourse in the home setting.

The side effects associated with intraurethral administration of alprostadil are similar to those associated with intracavernous injection. The primary complaint includes penile pain. Less often reported are side effects from systemic absorption. However, about 4 percent of the patients did have hypotension (low blood pressure).

In early 1997, patients across the country were treated with the intraurethral suppository (MUSE). Most were individuals who would have received intracavernous injection therapy with papaverine as the next step in their evaluation and treatment. The vast majority of patients say the gain is not worth the pain. In my own experience, less than 30 percent of patients had a satisfactory erection. No cases of penile fibrosis or priapism have been reported with the MUSE.[95]

As April of 1998 approached, most new patients who would normally have been treated with the MUSE suppository initially preferred to wait on the new oral Viagra. Today the intraurethral suppository plays a minor role in the treatment of patients with erectile dysfunction. When Viagra fails, some patients may think they prefer a urethral suppository over intracavernous injections. While a few patients may continue to need MUSE, most will move on to some other treatment model due to penile pain, lack of effectiveness, and cost ($140 for six pellets). The prescription refill rate for MUSE has been reported to be less than 20 percent.

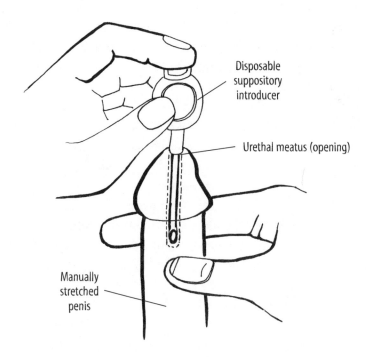

Disposable suppository introducer

Urethal meatus (opening)

Manually stretched penis

Fig. 7: Introduction of Urethal Suppository

9

T H E   P U M P

Vacuum Erection Devices

The vacuum erection device (recently renamed the vacuum constriction device) consists of a plastic cylinder that fits over the penis. This cylinder is connected either directly or by tubing to a vacuum generating source (a manual or a battery-operated pump). Once the penis is engorged with blood due to the negative pressure, a constricting ring is then applied to the base of the penis to maintain the erection [See Figure 8]. To minimize injury to the penis, the ring should not be left in place for longer than 30 minutes.

The erection resulting from a vacuum device is different from a natural spontaneous erection or one produced by intracavernous injection. First of all, that portion of the penis between the ring and the abdominal wall is not rigid. Sometimes this causes a lack of good base support and can result in a rotating, pivoting effect. After a few minutes the penile skin becomes cold and sometimes dusky. Also, ejaculation is different in that the semen usually goes retrograde as it is trapped by the constricting ring. Sometimes the ring can be uncomfortable or even painful. Some patients have additional numbness in the penis and develop bruising and bleeding below the skin (ecchymosis and petechiae). Men taking aspirin or Coumadin should exercise extreme caution when using these devices. The majority of men, on the other hand, did report satisfaction in terms of penile rigidity, length, and circumference.

They also reported good partner satisfaction.[96] These vacuum devices are contraindicated in patients with unexplained intermittent priapism and bleeding disorders.[97]

In patients with severe venous leakage or arterial insufficiency, fibrosis caused by priapism, or an infection from a prosthetic device, the vacuum device may not produce adequate erections. In those men, combining intracavernous injection with the vacuum erection device may enhance the erection.[98] The device may also be used successfully with men who have a malfunctioning penile implant in place.[99, 100]

The vacuum constriction device is much more acceptable to older males in a steady relationship than to the young single man. The young single male will have a much more difficult time explaining to his partner why he has to use the "mechanical oral sex device," as it was described by one patient.

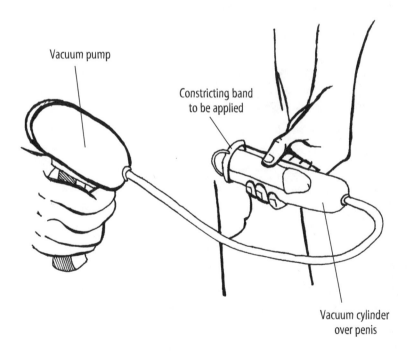

Vacuum pump

Constricting band
to be applied

Vacuum cylinder
over penis

Fig. 8: Vacuum Erection Device

10

T H E   K I N D E S T   C U T

Vascular Surgery for Erectile Dysfunction

Vascular surgery is a rarely needed or used treatment for erectile dysfunction but can be divided into two major areas: arterial revascularization of the penis, essentially repairing damaged vessels bringing blood into the penis; and surgery for veno-occlusive disorder, essentially correcting problems with the mechanics which clamp down on blood outflow. Several urological surgeons have contributed greatly to the development of surgical techniques for these vascular procedures, which are described in detail in medical literature that is widely read within urological specialties but does not need to be reviewed here.[101-106] Again, I want to stress that only rarely is an erectile dysfunction patient a candidate for even the specialized vascular testing that is available. Even more rare is the patient who should be offered the choice of vascular surgery.

Criteria for Evaluation for Penile Revascularization

Occasionally, a male patient's invasive x-rays (arteriogram) will reveal an isolated lesion on the pudendal artery in the pelvis. This will usually be a younger patient with a history of trauma, no history of diabetes, no history of smoking, and no history of any other underlying diseases such as systemic arteriosclerosis or veno-occlusive dysfunction. Such a patient may be a candidate for penile revascularization procedures. Practically no other patients will be.

In each region of the United States there are outstanding urologists who are dedicated to vascular microsurgical techniques. They are very good at their specialty, and the rest of us are not, so patients who need this type of treatment should probably be referred to one of five or six urologists in the country who are doing this type of procedure on a relatively larger volume than anyone else.

Color duplex doplar sonographic studies should be done before considering pudendal arteriography. Also, the second phase studies of Goldstein's dynamic infusion cavernosometry and cavernosography (DICC) should demonstrate functional arterial or venous disease. My experience is that the DICC studies should be done in the labs of the surgeons best capable of doing the surgery and limited to those referral centers. Patients who end up with a combination of arterial and veno-occlusive disease should be offered alternative choices, such as vacuum constriction devices, penile implants and, in more milder cases, vasoactive intracorporal injections.

Nevertheless, longterm success rates of 50 to 60 percent have been reported for penile revascularization and are considered by some to be less than optimal. The number of questions remain unanswered. Some reports have questioned the possible benefits from this type of vascular surgery.[105, 108-112]

Criteria for Surgery for Veno-Occlusive Disorder

The following criteria have been used for recommending a vascular procedure—usually a venous ligation procedure—to treat a veno-occlusive disorder: (1) a patient complaining of very short duration erections; (2) failure to initiate or maintain an erection from the intracavernous injection protocol with different agents and sexual stimulation; (3) normal cavernous arteries on the color duplex doplar studies or second phase of DICC; (4) determination of a faulty veno-occlusive mechanism as determined by a specific complex test—infusion pump or gravity cavernosometry; (5) location of the site of isolated venous leakage from the corpora cavernosa on cavernosography studies; (6) complete elimination of all tobacco use; (7) selection of this therapeutic approach after presentation to the patient of all alternative therapeutic choices as contrasted to the longterm success rate of 40 to 50 percent for venous surgery for treatment of erectile dysfunction.

Again, it should be emphasized that it is the rare patient who should even be offered this procedure. Even though veno-occlusion is a crucial part of the normal erection, there is no consensus that venous-occlusive surgery is a reasonable therapy. The three main arguments against this approach include:

(1) Venous occlusion is dependent on arterial inflow and relaxation of the smooth muscle in the erectile cylinders; therefore, it is possible that poor venous-occlusion may reflect a problem with the sinoid smooth muscle. There is no current way to evaluate, diagnose, and treat damage to the smooth muscle.

(2) There is still controversy as to the type of test and sequence of tests best utilized to diagnose veno-occlusive disorders.

(3) There is wide variation in surgical results and longterm return to normal potency following this surgery, probably due to a variety of surgical techniques. An accurate comparison of results using different surgical techniques has been difficult.

Plain Talk Summary of Vascular Surgery for Erectile Dysfunction

Over the past 15 years great strides have been made in attempting to revascularize the penis in individuals with arterial occlusion or leakage of blood from the venous drainage system of the erectile cylinders (veno-occlusive disorders). Longterm results have been less than satisfactory with only about 50 percent of the patients having satisfactory outcomes. Arterial revascularization may have a very limited role in those rare individuals with congenital vascular occlusions or in young males with obstructed, isolated arteries secondary to trauma. Less well-understood are the key factors that influence a good outcome with veno-occlusive surgery.[113] As with arterial revascularization, the longterm postoperative outcome of venous surgery is generally poor.[114] While there are a few patients with localized lesions who are excellent candidates for revascularization, the surgery should be offered only to the very rare patient. The procedure should be limited to those individual urologists and referral centers who are doing research and developing new techniques and who have the most experience with the vascular corrective procedures.

11

"THE CADILLAC"

Overview of Penile Implants

The history of the development of the penile prosthesis for the treatment of impotence goes back to experience gained from trauma surgeons' treatment of men who required reconstruction of the penis following severe accident or injury. The first reported successful reconstruction used rib cartilage implanted into a graft fashioned out of skin and formed into a tube that was placed in the location of the normal penis.[115]

The apparent inspiration for making a prosthesis from rib cartilage was the observation that many animals have a bone in the penis that assists with erections. In nature, these bones begin as a pair of cartilages in the penis.[116] These cartilages subsequently fuse into a bone-like structure referred to as the os penis. The os penis is quite variable in its location and function and size in nature.[117] Even Aristotle made note of the "littlestick," referring to the os penis in the fox and wolf.[116] During World War II, soldiers who suffered traumatic penile loss in battle were treated with reconstructive procedures utilizing a rib segment to provide rigidity and support for the penis.[118] Further refining this technique, Bergman and coworkers in the United States in 1948 reported a four-stage plastic surgery procedure for creation of a penis using cartilage from the eighth or ninth rib.[116] With today's microvascular techniques, plastic and reconstructive surgeons are able to get good results by using vascularized myocutaneous flaps, thus avoiding multi-staged procedures.

Early Synthetic Penile Inserts

By the late 1940s and early 1950s, it was well-recognized that cartilage had disadvantages for penile inserts, being often found to either be too short or have too great a curvature to function successfully.[119] This led Goodwin and Scott to use specially shaped acrylic splints as penile implants in a nonreconstructive setting for the management of impotence for the first time.[119] On the other hand, these splints were not placed inside the corpus cavernosum. Others used perforated acrylic rods for treatment of impotence with the similar placement in the top part of the penis between the two corpus cavernosum, referring to this location of the acrylic rods as creating an "artificial os penis."[120, 121]

During the 1950s complications with acrylic rods placed outside the corpora cavernosa became evident, including perforations and ulcerations. In 1958, Beheri began using two separate polyethylene rods placed inside the corpus cavernosal space as rigid stents.[122, 123] This placement seemed superior in suppleness and malleability to the earlier placement of the rods outside the corporus cavernosal tissue. In 1966 Beheri reported longterm results with over 700 patients, presenting a surgical technique for the intracavernous placement of his polyethylene rods much in the fashion that we place prosthetic cylinders today.[124]

In the late 1960s, silicone became popular for prostheses due to its qualities: it induced minimal tissue reaction, it was unbreakable, had a nice mix of rigidity and resiliency, and could be bent to allow easier surgical insertion. [125-127] Silicone was first tried outside the corpus cavernosum between Buck's fascia and the tunica albuginea. There was a considerable degree of instability, pain and actual extrusion through the skin or the urethra.[126, 127] However, when the silicone rubber cylinders were placed within the erectile cylinders, they conformed more to the normal tumescent form of the penis and provided satisfactory vaginal penetration without interfering with normal daily activities and without being uncomfortable with most clothing.[127] In the 1970s we saw the introduction of the two broad categories of penile implants which are still utilized today: the semirigid or malleable prosthesis and the multi-component inflatable prosthesis.

Semi-Rigid Rod Prosthesis

Small and his workers introduced the Small-Carrion device in the early seventies as a pair of sponge-filled silicone prosthetic cylinders to be implanted inside the natural erectile cylinders.[128] This device was later modified by Finney[129] with a hinge section allowing for penile flexion at the pubic level. This was subsequently modified by Jonas with a prosthesis consisting of silicone rubber with a core of twisted silver wire, enabling the bending of the prosthesis into any desired position.[130] When one combines the above-mentioned prosthesis with the American Medical Systems (AMS) malleable prosthesis and the Mentor malleable prosthesis, one has the current list of available semirigid and malleable prosthesis available for implantation today. American Medical Systems devices are very straightforward as far as their surgical implantation and often can be implanted with just local anesthesia.[131] The primary disadvantage of this device is that it is not as natural as the inflatable device in that the penis stays the same degree of rigidity all the time. This lack of going from flaccid to rigid is one of the reasons that the inflatable device was developed. In addition, those patients who require inspection of the bladder and surgery on the bladder or prostate transurethrally will have problems with that procedure due to the difficulty in the introduction of surgical instruments into the urethra with the semirigid rod prosthesis cylinders occupying the space in the erectile cylinders, as well. It just gets too crowded to do cystoscopic procedures on those patients with semi-rigid rod implants. To overcome some of these difficulties the inflatable device was developed along with the goal of making the device much more natural in its function.

Inflatable Prostheses

In 1973, F. Brantley Scott and coworkers first described their initial use of an implantable inflatable penile prosthesis.[132] This initial Scott prosthesis consisted of two silicone rubber cylinders composed of Dacron-reinforced silicone. This device also included a reservoir with saline solution as the inflation medium for this hydraulic device. The pump, controlled by external squeezing, was located in the subcutaneous tissue in the scrotum. Originally, Dr. Scott's research had been geared toward the evaluation and management of incontinent (lacking urination control) patients. He first developed a prosthetic device including an inflatable balloon that goes around the urinary tract at the neck of the bladder or around the urethra in the penis. A quarter-century later, this device is implanted to control incontinence in thousands of patients each year. Dr. Scott's "artificial urinary sphincter" has been a major contribution to the management of urinary incontinence.

However, one of Scott's colleagues suggested that he take the inflatable balloon used for the artificial urinary sphincter and straighten it out and put it in the corpus cavernosum as an inflatable penile implant. Using two of these inflatable cylinders, Scott thus started the management with an inflatable device. This device was manufactured by American Medical Systems, a company founded to support research and development of prosthetic devices for urology, including Dr. Scott's work at Baylor College of Medicine in Houston. Over the past 15 years, the inflatable penile prosthesis, produced by AMS, has been improved and modified, and a lot of the early kinks in the hydraulic device worked out to the point where today it is a very reliable device.

The three-piece American Medical Systems 700 series device has a choice of two different cylinders. The 700-CX cylinders are heavier-duty cylinders that expand just in girth, or width, and is particularly helpful for diabetic patients with a lot of fibrosis of the wall of the corpus cavernosum, as well as for patients with Peyronie's disease. The AMS 700-Ultrex cylinders have been available since 1990 and expand in both girth and length, producing a more comfortable fit in the deflated stage. Mentor Corporation also makes an inflatable device that works well.

My own personal experience with implants has been limited to the AMS products since I had the opportunity to train with Dr. Brantley Scott in the late 1970s and early 1980s. The inflatable device was intended to mimic much more closely the natural erection. When the cylinders are deflated, the penis is flaccid, and when one activates the scrotal pump, fluid is transferred into the inflatable cylinders and the penis becomes erect [See Figure 9]. With the inflatable device, no one is able to tell that the patient has a prosthesis in place. On the other hand, as Dr. Scott used to say, there is a "locker room" benefit, because with the inflatable cylinders in place, even when they are deflated, the flaccid penis has an increased degree of fullness and length.

Self-Contained Inflatable and Mechanical Penile Prosthesis

To combine the desired flaccid penis achievable with the inflatable devices while at the same time having a much more simple device, like the semirigid rods, the self-contained inflatable mechanical devices were developed, such as the currently used Ambicor or Duraphase devices. When the Ambicor device is deflated, it's not quite as flaccid as the AMS-700 ultrex cylinders, for example. Also, when the Ambicor is inflated, one simply has a semirigid rod-type girth and the Ambicor does not increase further in girth nor any in length.

Cost used to be a problem when very few insurance companies covered the device and there was a difference in the amount of time in a hospital between the semirigid rod devices, which were done as outpatient, versus the inflatable devices that were done with a several-day hospital stay. Now all of these devices are implanted on an outpatient basis and when insurance companies cover the device, they cover all of them equally. If the patient has Medicare or Blue Cross, the devices are covered. With increasing numbers of managed care and HMOs we are beginning to see some restrictions on coverage for this type of prosthetic procedures. The best advice to anyone who is diabetic or who has had radical prostate cancer surgery and may well need an implant later on is to be certain that your particular HMO or managed care plan covers this form of treatment before enrolling in that plan. One insurance company, Mail Handlers Insurance, has universally not covered anything related to erectile dysfunction or sexual dysfunction evaluation and treatment. This insurance is what most of our postal workers have as their health insurance.

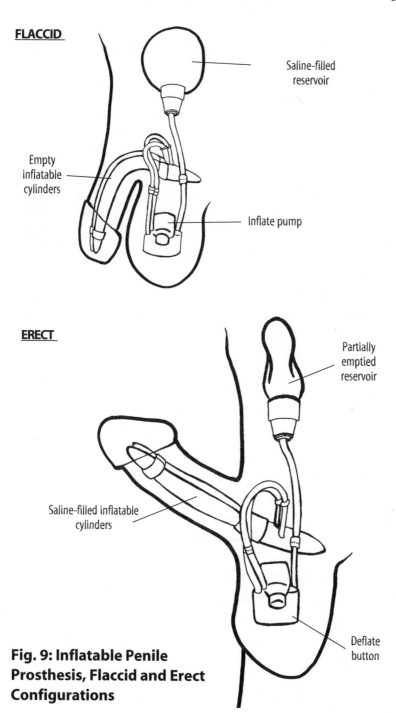

FLACCID

Saline-filled reservoir

Empty inflatable cylinders

Inflate pump

ERECT

Partially emptied reservoir

Saline-filled inflatable cylinders

Deflate button

Fig. 9: Inflatable Penile Prosthesis, Flaccid and Erect Configurations

Making the Decision for Penile Implant Surgery

Since the availability of penile prosthesis surgery, the most difficult aspect for patients and their partners is the decision to go ahead with the surgery. This has been a difficulty for patients for the last 25 years. Even though they are aware they've tried every possible other alternative to surgery, often it does take awhile for them to make the decision. It's important from the physician's standpoint to make sure that the patient understands that none of these penile implants will restore the full length the patient was previously able to achieve with his natural erection. It's also important for the patients to understand the advantages and disadvantages of all types of implants and that the patient's preference be the number one priority. The surgeon's preference is probably the number two priority. However, often we as surgeons tend to steer the patients toward our favorite operative procedure. Frequently, the males make the decision to go ahead and have the implant and just plan to surprise their partner or simply do it over her concerns. This is often the case when the partner has not been involved in the office visits and workup and treatment decisions in the office.

I can always tell when the patient made this decision on his own when I visit the waiting room after doing the implant surgery only to have the wife comment: "I tried to talk Charlie out of it" or "This was all his idea, not mine." Occasionally, the patient's wife feels they have to apologize for Charlie deciding on his own to have the implant procedure as if return to normal sexual function is taboo at Charlie's age. For the most part, however, the problem lies with Charlie in those situations in that he has not insisted on having his wife in on the decision-making and his wife is not fully informed as to the risk of surgery nor to the advantages and disadvantages of the device. Most wives, however, are genuinely concerned about their husband's satisfactory tolerance of the surgery and his safety back in the recovery room when we speak to them after surgery. Occasionally, the patient with a penile implant will have some psychological adjustment to make at home in that before surgery Charlie was a docile, snoozing house cat on the sofa, but once the implant is in place, he subsequently turns into an aggressive tiger. In those situations the clinical psychologist working with the couple can help with the adjustment after surgery.

Sometimes it helps individuals make the decision to go ahead with surgery if they have an opportunity to discuss the surgery with individuals who have already had the implant. Patients may have the opportunity to discuss all ramifications of the surgery with others who have already had the implant at regularly scheduled impotency support groups [See Chapter 14]. The vast majority of patients do not need to speak to someone else before making the decision, but if they've been in attendance at the support group meetings, they certainly are well-prepared for the implant surgery.

Success Rate

Overall success rate with penile implants is excellent. Patient satisfaction ranges from 80 to 97 percent. In the short term in the first few months after surgery the main risk is that of infection. The infection rate is about 2 percent and when an infection occurs, the best management is to remove the prosthesis and treat the infection and replace the prosthesis in six to nine months once the patient has no signs of infection and the tissue has adequately healed in the area of the surgery. There have been successful instances where the surgeon did what's called a rescue operation where, in the face of infection, the first implanted device is removed and the tissue irrigated with copious amounts of antibiotic solutions and a new device implanted. A recent report of a study involving a large series of patients found good success and decreased long-term morbidity with this technique.[134]

Malfunction of the device varies from device to device and a lot of the studies that have been done to assess the long-term-life expectancy of the prosthesis from a malfunction standpoint have been retrospective studies. In general, the malfunction rate is about 5 percent over a ten-year period for most implantable devices. This means that after ten years 95 percent of the patients will have had no problems.

Those individuals who have a malfunction usually have a leakage of fluid from one of the inflatable cylinders or a loose tubing connector. They can have the implant revised during a second operative procedure, again as an outpatient.

With a revision procedure, the risk of infection goes up as does the risk of another malfunction. The risk of infection is as high as 10 percent in some studies with a revision procedure and the risk of another malfunction from the loss of fluid, from whatever source, is about 10 percent. The majority of patients are well satisfied with their inflatable penile prosthesis and would undergo an operative procedure every few years if necessary to continue to have it function well.

Fortunately, with the current devices and with the improvements that American Medical Systems and also Mentor Corporation have made in the older devices, the revision rates have been reduced substantially. Incidentally, nowhere in the prosthesis is silicone gel utilized. Prospective studies are underway and our practice is participating in one of the prospective studies for the FDA looking at safety as well as efficacy of the AMS inflatable penile prostheses. This particular study will help generate some long-term data in a prospective rather than retrospective fashion.

Plain Talk Summary on Penile Implants

Penile implants are a well-established successful method of treating erectile dysfunction. While this treatment option should be utilized only after other current nonsurgical treatment options have been exhausted, it should not be looked upon as a last resort. While the procedure is not without a very small risk of infection and a small risk of malfunction due to leakage of fluid from one of the inflatable devices over time, the overall patient and partner satisfaction rates are very high. Prior to surgery the patient and his partner should have realistic expectations as to the role of the penile implant. For example, its primary function is to make the penis rigid. This will not solve relationship problems, financial problems, or other issues that may be contributing to psychological sexual dysfunction.

Patients also need to understand that no penile prosthesis will provide the full length previously achieved by the patient with his natural erection. Once patients make the difficult decision to proceed with the penile implant after all other options have failed them, they usually comment several months after surgery that they wish the procedure had been done six months to a year earlier. Currently, long-term prospective studies are underway in order to fully evaluate the safety and efficiency of the currently utilized inflatable penile prosthesis.

12

A CROOKED TALE

Treatment of Peyronie's Disease

As discussed in Chapter 3, Peyronie's disease is the result of an often painful inflammation of the wall of the erectile cylinders of the penis. Usually, this involves the formation of scar tissue, or plaque, along the top of the penis. The scarring causes the penis to curve upward or to the side. How physicians treat Peyronie's disease depends on the degree of difficulty the individual is having with side effects of the inflammation. The overall goals are to reduce the initial pain involved with the acute inflammatory phase, to decrease penile curvature when it is causing a functional problem with erections, and to restore normal erectile function where the patient has inadequate erections, usually in combination with a severe curvature deformity.

Natural Course of the Disease

We have known for a long time that the acute inflammatory phase of Peyronie's disease may last up to 12 months. Therefore, conservative nonsurgical management should be used for the first year. In the past we have correlated the acute painful phase with the acute inflammatory process; however, pain does not always have to be present for there to be progressive scarring. One retrospective review found up to 40 percent of Peyronie's patients experienced progressive problems with curvature and erectile dysfunction from the date the patient first came to the physician, usually complaining of painful erections or penile curvature. Up to 30 percent of the patients had spontaneous improvement of their symptoms during the ensuing 12 months. Also of interest in this particular study was the fact that there was no significant difference in outcome between those who were treated with drugs and those who received no treatment.[135] During the first 12 months, while waiting for the acute inflammation to settle down, some patients that have used intracavernous injections or the vacuum constriction device for treatment of the erection portion of the problem have actually seen an increase in the penile curvature.[136]

Medical Management

For a number of years, oral medications have been the popular treatment by urologists for patients when they first present with penile pain, plaque formation, curvature with erections, hourglass deformity or erectile dysfunction. The two most common oral agents are Vitamin E and potassium para-aminobenzoate (POTABA). The Vitamin E, at 400 IU twice a day, is inexpensive with no side effects. In some retrospective studies it appears to be successful in some patients. In like manner, results with POTABA have mostly been reported in a retrospective fashion. Up to two-thirds of patients get a significant decrease in penile pain, shrinking of the Peyronie's plaque, and decrease in the penile curvature over a six-month span of oral therapy. On the other hand, the POTABA is much more expensive, since 12 grams per day are required. Usually 24 tablets per day are taken at a dose of 500 mg. per tablet. The patient must balance the cost of the drug against the reports that 30 percent of the Peyronie's patients will see a spontaneous improvement without taking any medication. Nevertheless, most patients who are having painful erections or a significant curvature do want to try some type of therapy, and are usually started on either Vitamin E or POTABA.

A number of researchers have tried injecting the Peyronie's plaque with drugs aimed at decreasing the fibrosis early in the plaque formation stage. For example, Gelbard and associates[137] did a careful prospective randomized study with the injection of collagenase directly into the

Peyronie's plaque. They found no statistically significant decrease of penile curvature following these injections. Nor have intralesion injections of steroids resulted in any measurable, significant success. Levine and coworkers[138] have injected calcium channel blockers into Peyronie's plaques, and have reported a decrease in the scar process and subsequent fibrosis in some patients. On the other hand, this technique failed to alleviate the curvature. Radiation therapy in low doses has been used on patients in extremely rare cases where the painful phase has been very protracted. However, these individuals need to be aware that radiation can cause additional damaging fibrosis inside the corpus cavernosum.[139]

Surgical Treatment

Fortunately, the vast majority of patients with Peyronie's disease do not have deformity severe enough to require surgery, which should be reserved for those with the most severe deformities and erectile dysfunction. If surgery is considered, the inflammatory process needs to be stable, and in most cases the patient will have been monitored for at least 12 months from their initial symptoms.

• The first of three groups of operative procedures involves either a *plication procedure* or the *Nesbitt procedure*. Individuals with mild to moderate curvature but no erectile dysfunction are candidates for these procedures. Since either procedure will cause a small degree of penile shortening, the patient needs to have adequate penile length. With the plication procedure, the surgeon makes an incision in the area of the penis opposite the curvature to do a counter-straightening procedure when the incision is closed in a transverse fashion. The Nesbitt modification is usually used for patients with more significant curvature. Again, these patients must have good blood flow and normal erectile function out distal to the Peyronie's plaque portion of the penis. In the Nesbitt procedure, an ellipse of the tunica albuginea is removed opposite the point of the greatest curvature. This incision is then closed with permanent, nonabsorbable sutures. Most of these patients get a very good result and are able to return to normal sexual function.[140]

• The next surgical procedure involves either incision or excision of the Peyronie's plaque along with placement of a graft to cover the ensuing defect in the corpus cavernosum. Patients who are candidates for this procedure will have enough curvature to prevent intercourse but will otherwise have good erectile function. Often these patients will have the severe hourglass type deformity and a short penis. Since the previously discussed plication or Nesbitt techniques shortens the penis, the patient who has a short penis to begin with would not be a candidate for plication, but may be a candidate for plaque incision and grafting. Several different materials have been used over the years for the graft. Since 1974 Divine and Horton[141] have used a dermal (skin) graft to cover the deformity left where the plaque is incised or excised. Lue[142] reported using saphenous vein to create a vein graft patch. He has reported good success with this material. Synthetic materials, such as woven Dacron or Gortex, have been used, but produce poor longterm elasticity when compared with dermal or saphenous vein patches. Erectile dysfunction rates following plaque excision or incision and graft placement have been reported to be as high as 65 to 70 percent. Following this procedure some patients will have a decreased penile sensation, recurrent curvature problems or progressive erectile dysfunction.

• The last type of surgical procedure for the Peyronie's patient who has severe curvature involves penile prosthesis implants, with or without excision of the plaque. In the late seventies and early eighties it was fashionable to try a one-stage operation where the implant was placed and the plaque excised and a woven Dacron graft utilized to cover the excision. However, those patients had to remain hospitalized for up to a week and the post-op infection rate was significantly higher than the 2 percent infection rate associated with doing the penile implant procedure alone. In the early eighties, in an effort to reduce the risk of infection, I used a two-stage procedure on a series of patients with severe Peyronie's disease requiring implant surgery. The first stage would be implantation of the prosthesis, with plans to come back in several months and do a straightening operation where needed. I prefer to use the AMS 700-CX cylinders for patients with Peyronie's disease. These are the "heavy duty" cylinders in our armament of prosthetic cylinders.

While the 700-CX cylinder expands in girth only, I have found that over time the plaque will stretch and the patient can actually mold the penis back to straightness, usually within six months after implantation. Anecdotally, I've had a couple of patients with a U-configuration of the penis after the cylinders were implanted, due to their Peyronie's scarring causing an upward curve of the penis. The penis actually curved to the point where the tip touched the abdominal wall. Within six months those patients were in the office with 95 percent straightened penises, just by inflating the prosthesis and working on bending the penis toward the normal plane. Other urologists have reported a great deal of success by giving attention to the plaque at the time of the implant procedure.[143] This technique involves having the surgeon bend the penis in the direction opposite the curvature when the penile prosthesis cylinders are inflated. The penis is held in that position during surgery for a couple of minutes in order to lyse some of the plaque and help stretch the plaque at that time. Whether working on the plaque in the operating room or having a patient do the stretching of the plaque postoperatively, the results are excellent. Rarely does a graft have to be used today, which certainly cuts down the cost since the implant procedure is routinely done on an outpatient basis versus one week in the hospital to recover from the combined implantation and plaque excision with grafting that was popular in the late seventies and early eighties

Plain Talk Summary: Treatment of Peyronie's Disease

The current treatment of Peyronie's disease depends on the patient's symptoms, being mindful that the acute inflammatory phase may take up to 12 months to subside. Initial treatment uses oral medications to help reduce pain, reduce penile curvature, and shrink the plaque that forms along the top of the penis. Once the inflammation has stabilized, the the vast majority of patients will not need surgery. Potential surgery patients need to understand that the inflammation resulting in scar and plaque formation will shorten the penis, and that none of the surgical procedures can return the penis back to its pre-Peyronie's length. Patients with minimal curvature and normal erections frequently state that they are happy and don't want any surgery. If they do want to see an improvement in the curvature, the more conservative Nesbitt procedure, or corpus cavernosum plication, is a good choice. On the other hand, if the patient has a short penis and a very severe curvature with normal erectile function, incising or excising the plaque with a dermal or vein patch graft is a good choice. Most patients with severe curvature will have significant erectile dysfunction and are best served with an inflatable penile prosthesis implant. This is usually done on an outpatient basis and with excellent results in a one-stage procedure without having to incise or excise the plaque. The two most important facts to remember about Peyronie's disease are, first, the majority of patients will not need surgery and, secondly, there is no standard treatment protocol; every patient is treated individually.

13

M A T T E R   O V E R   M I N D

Treatment of
Psychological Erectile Dysfunction

I n the 1960s and early 1970s psychogenic or psychological factors were thought to be the cause for 90 percent of male erectile dysfunction. Today, we realize that purely psychogenic causes account for no more than 15 percent of the men with this problem. However, it is rare indeed to see a man with a physical cause of erectile dysfunction who does not also complain of a marked psychological impact. Therefore psychosexual therapy for impotence divides into two groups of patients: those whose underlying problem is primarily psychological, and those whose underlying problem is primarily physical. .

Psychosexual Therapy for Organic Erectile Dysfunction

Over the last 25 years urologists have learned that as men with primarily physical, or organic, erectile dysfunction have their underlying physical problem treated, regardless of the method of treatment, the associated psychological effects (performance anxiety, fear of failure, depression resulting in decreased libido) will usually work themselves out by the time the physical problem is fully treated. For a number of men with organic erectile dysfunction, psychosexual therapy is very useful in relieving anxiety and helping to remove unrealistic expectations from the particular surgical or medical treatment,[144] especially where penile implants are used. On the other hand, when physical causes are involved, psychotherapy alone rarely corrects erectile dysfunction. A report of psychotherapy alone with diabetic males whose underlying problem was organically based erectile dysfunction, helps place the role of psychotherapy alone into better perspective.[145] In that particular study, only 15 percent of diabetic males with a physical erectile dysfunction problem had a long-term improvement after treatment with just psychotherapy.[145]

Psychotherapy for Psychogenic Erectile Dysfunction

In general, there are two categories of psychotherapy: psychoanalytic therapy and symptom-oriented counseling. The principles of psychoanalytic individual therapy assume that sexual dysfunction is a manifestation of an underlying subconscious conflict, and psychoanalytical principles are used to treat the anxiety that has resulted from that subconscious conflict. Today, most psychologists, psychiatrists, and urologists would agree that psychoanalytical therapy is rarely the right approach. But, a symptom-oriented approach has been used extensively by both psychologists and urologists. The main components of this approach include reassurance, encouragement, providing a full explanation of the cause of the symptoms, and providing sexual information both to the patient and his partner. It is very important to have the partner involved in this therapeutic approach.

Sex Therapy

In the 1970s Masters and Johnson described their approach for the treatment of erectile dysfunction with the elimination of self-observation and self-evaluation during sexual activity.[19] The sex therapists would ask the patient to engage in no activity except as directed by the therapist. They would then instruct the couple in initiating physical contact solely for the purpose of producing pleasurable physical sensation, and not for the purpose of forcing sexual arousal and intercourse. They emphasize the non-goal-oriented approach. The therapist gave the couple an opportunity to focus on pleasurable physical sensations, rather than on performance. The directive not to engage in sexual activity helped alleviate some of the performance pressures. The therapists' aim was to detach sexuality from performance anxiety, inhibition, and guilt. As the couple became more comfortable with the sensory focus exercises, they gradually progressed to direct genital stimulation done in a non-demanding and non-goal-oriented way. During this stage of treatment the man was likely to get an erection. He was instructed to discontinue stimulation and allow the erection to subside before continuing. This helped him realize that getting and maintaining an erection is a natural process which does not require a conscious effort. This is an important point since most males with performance anxiety tend to be goal-directed individuals who try to force an erection to occur rather than letting it happen naturally. As erections increased in frequency and the man became more confident, the couple was instructed to incorporate intercourse into their sexual activity. Modifications to the Masters and Johnson technique have been made, for example, with Kaplan emphasizing the treatment underlying personal or interpersonal conflicts.[146, 147]

Most patients with psychological erectile dysfunction do not require the complex Masters and Johnson type treatment described above. The best therapy is simply to encourage the couple to abstain from intercourse for a selected period during which they are instructed to avoid the demands for performance and to focus on producing pleasure rather than arousal. On their own they're instructed not to have intercourse while allowing any erections that occur to subside before stimulation is resumed. The man is, for example, given specific instructions to concentrate on the physical sensations he's experiencing and to be aware of his partner's response rather than to focus on his erection. Then, as the man increases his self-confidence, the couple may be able to resume intercourse with relative ease.

Hengeveld[144] has listed a number of contraindications for psychosexual therapy. These include the patient who is very uncooperative or who has an uncooperative sexual partner. Obviously, effective sex therapy requires a very cooperative couple.

Other contraindications include a male with low sex drive; a documented psychosis or a major mood disorder which needs to be addressed first; and major interpersonal problems with the sexual partner.

In the latter instance, the relationship needs to be fixed before addressing the erectile dysfunction secondary to performance anxiety. If a couple cannot stand to be in the same room with each other, it's unlikely they're going to be able to cooperate in one of the psychosexual therapies. Finally, once individual couples fail psychosexual treatment, it's going to be difficult to expect results in the future with additional psychosexual treatment. Initially, in 1970, Masters and Johnson reported a 70 percent success rate in restoring erectile dysfunction. Subsequently, other reports have ranged down to as low as 30 to 35 percent success.[144]

In the early 1970s the choices for treatment of erectile dysfunction, whether primarily physical or primarily psychogenic in origin, were between psychosexual therapy and penile implantation. Since the therapeutic gulf between these two treatments was so wide, individuals with primarily psychogenic impotence who were candidates for a penile implant had to have the express approval and recommendation from their psychiatrist after having failed a genuine effort at sex therapy. As direct intracavernous injection therapy, along with the use of vacuum erection devices, became popular in the early eighties, we as clinicians then had other alternative, minimally invasive treatments to offer patients who failed psychosexual therapy or who preferred not to undergo psychosexual therapy protocols. The main advantage, for example, of intracavernous injection is that the results are prompt. Usually, within a few weeks the patient with psychogenic impotence will be able to achieve satisfactory erections, following the injection of one of the vasoactive drugs, about ten minutes after injection. Up to 60 percent of men with primarily performance anxiety will gradually become less dependent on the injection, and finally reach a point where they can leave off the injections and have adequate, spontaneous erections. This proves to be a cheaper form of therapy compared to multiple visits with the sex therapist.

In my practice today, I rarely have to refer a patient whose problem is primarily psychogenic in origin to a psychologist or sex therapist.

In many instances, patients with erectile dysfunction secondary to life events, that were summarized in Chapter 3, will see a gradual disappearance of the problem over time as the triggering event recedes. The duration of these transient erectile difficulties is often proportional to the degree of trauma of the precipitating event. There's no specific guideline for how long to wait before doing more than just reassuring the patient and being understanding. Each individual patient has to be treated and their problem addressed on an individual basis. One of the problems with all of these approaches to psychological counseling and behavior modification-type therapy is the lack of good documentation of success rates for specific techniques.[17]

Plain Talk Summary: Treatment of Psychogenic Erectile Dysfunction

Since the vast majority of males with erectile dysfunction have an underlying physical cause, treatment of that physical problem and correction of the physical source of their erectile dysfunction will usually resolve the psychogenic component. But very few patients with a physical cause to their erectile dysfunction will see an improvement from only psychosexual therapy, counseling, and behavior modification protocols. On the other hand, those individuals with a primarily psychololigal cause, regardless of the underlying precipitating factors, usually respond today to one of the minimally invasive treatments — vacuum erection devices, urethral suppositories, or intracavernous injection of vasoactive drugs, and now Viagra. The sex therapy techniques of Masters and Johnson from the 1960s and '70s and the later modifications of that approach are usually not necessary today.

Many patients with primarily psychological effects due to a recent life event, such as the death of a family member or personal stresses at work or in their marriage will see a return to normal erectile function once the relationship problems in their marriage are resolved, or an adequate amount of time has passed since their traumatic loss of a family member. The key to treating psychogenic erectile dysfunction is to involve the patient's partner in the treatment. It's important for the partner, as well as the physician, to be supportive. Fortunately, today we have other choices than the penile implant for psychogenic erectile dysfunction in those individuals who fail counseling and psychotherapy. As we better understand the physiology of normal erectile function, additional nonsurgical options will become available for those individuals with a purely psychogenic etiology. More research is needed in the treatment of individuals with psychogenic erectile dysfunction, comparing all of the currently available treatment modalities in controlled studies.

14

POTENCY RESTORED

Role of Impotence Support Groups

Support groups for individuals with erectile dysfunction became popular in the early 1980s. These groups were referred to as impotence support groups because impotence was the term commonly used, instead of "erectile dysfunction," at that time. The role of any support group is to provide individuals, or couples, with encouragement, advice, educational information, and compassionate support, usually provided by individuals and couples who have had the same problem and been able to overcome their individual medical, psychological, or relationship problem. The support groups for individuals and couples with erectile dysfunction are no different than those for other medical problems. Support groups are composed of two groups of individuals, those who have had a particular problem and been able to have that problem treated, usually successfully, and individuals with a problem who are very early in their diagnosis, workup, and treatment. Those individuals who have had their problem treated successfully, therefore, from a personal experience standpoint, can provide advice and encouragement to the individuals who have yet to undergo treatment. As we all know, some illnesses require more than one operation or one round of medication. For example, in the management of chronic alcoholism the alcoholic support groups, Alcoholics Anonymous, have played a major role in helping individuals manage their chronic problem.

The goals of a support group for patients suffering with erectile dysfunction are no different than the goals of support groups for other illnesses. In the group setting, individuals who have had an erectile dysfunction problem that has been successfully managed are available to provide support, counsel, encouragement in a confidential, casual setting. Most support groups are composed of a urologist, psychologist, and someone from the education department of a community hospital, which is where most of the support groups across the country hold their meetings. Since the goal is educational, most hospitals are willing to provide a meeting place.

Meetings usually last 60 to 90 minutes. The first part of the meeting is usually a presentation, lecture, panel discussion, or a brief video of some aspect of erectile dysfunction. Popular topics for the first part of the presentation include: overview of causes and treatment of erectile dysfunction, surgical treatments for erectile dysfunction, nonsurgical treatments for erectile dysfunction, medications that cause erectile dysfunction, the role of hormonal management for erectile dysfunction, psychogenic causes and treatment of erectile dysfunction, and panel discussion of treatment outcomes.

Probably the most important part of the support group program is the informal meeting time after the opening lecture or presentation. During this one-on-one time, individuals have the opportunity to meet with other men who have had their erectile dysfunction problem solved by penile implantation surgery, or any of the nonsurgical treatments, including the recent use of Viagra. Those individuals who have failed all nonsurgical treatments, and are considering a penile implant at this point, have the opportunity to talk to other individuals and other couples where the implant has corrected and solved their erectile dysfunction. As mentioned earlier, the most difficult part about having a penile implant making the decision to go ahead with surgery once all other treatment options have been unsuccessful.

In the early 1980s when impotence support groups first became fashionable, the treatment options were very limited. These early group sessions focused primarily on all of the ramifications of penile implant surgery along with the importance of the relationship and how to manage performance anxiety. Patients undergoing penile implant surgery are always much better informed of what to expect when they have the opportunity to discuss this operation and its outcome with other men who have had the surgery.

Fifteen years ago, we began a support group, "Potency Restored," in Montgomery, Alabama, where my practice is located. Over the period, a number of additional nonsurgical treatments have evolved. Patients do not always want or need the advice and counsel of someone who has already been there before they take oral medication, such as Viagra, or use the vacuum erection device, or do self-injections with vasoactive drugs. On the other hand, when one's treatment or management is only marginally successful, attending the "Potency Restored" group meetings helps them with their current treatment, and also enlightens them as to the other options for treatment. We encourage the men in the group to bring their spouse to the support group meetings. Couples now make up about 30 percent of the regular attendees.

Over the past 15 years, a large number of couples who have participated in the "Potency Restored" group have come back to the meetings year after year. Not only have they contributed valuable information to the new attendees, but they have actually made friends and converted the meetings into somewhat of a family affair. In fact, some of the members don't make the monthly meetings throughout the year on a very regular basis, but they make a maximum effort to attend the group's annual Christmas party. "Potency Restored," as with other support groups, is all about people helping other people.

Memorable Moments at "Potency Restored" Meetings

Some memorable moments have occurred in our group meetings over the past decade and a half. Dr. Taz Jones, a clinical psychologist and frequent participant in our meetings, one night showed up with two, six-foot ladders, two concrete blocks, and one eight-foot 2x4 board. At first I thought he had gotten lost on his way to do some handy work around his house, but he quickly told me all of his props were relevant for his discussion that evening. We had previously stressed to the group that performance anxiety is a common part of erectile dysfunction and happens to just about everyone with a physical cause to their problem. To dramatize how performance anxiety can affect any task, Dr. Jones did a simple demonstration. He placed his 2x4 on the floor in front of the group and asked for volunteers. Three gentlemen near the front came up, and each easily walked across the board without falling off. Dr. Jones then raised the board about eight inches off the floor by placing it across the two concrete blocks. At this point one of the volunteers declined to even try a walk on the board, while the other two walked, but with a lot less confidence than before. Dr. Jones then suspended the board between the second steps on the two ladders. Needless to say, none of the three volunteers wanted to walk the plank when it was three feet off the floor. He asked them, what was the difference? It was the same board. It was as sturdy off the floor as it had been before. The difference, obviously, was now the three men were each beginning to think about what they were doing. One said he was afraid he would fall and break an ankle. Another said he had had problems with his hip and might not be able to balance as well. The third was afraid his insurance wouldn't cover any injury associated with such a stunt.

Dr. Jones had gotten his point across. Each of his volunteers had developed quite a bit of performance anxiety brought on by worry about, "what would happen if." While we do not want patients to think that having an erection is a performance—in fact, we want just the opposite—each of these men did develop performance anxiety. When it comes to an erection, we know that we can't just demand the penis to perform. In addition, the more one thinks about having an erection, thinks about what will happen if they can't perform, the more likely it is that their natural erection will go away.

Male Bashing

When given the opportunity in open discussions on the topic of romance, the ladies in the audience at our "Potency Restored" meetings in Montgomery frequently do a bit of male bashing. A typical example occurred during a panel discussion program where two couples were answering questions from the audience in round-table fashion. I was the moderator. The men had both had penile implants for at least four years. The wives attested to the positive effects of the implant and said that their husbands were no longer depressed and they had basically seen a total turnaround in their husbands' personalities once their erectile dysfunction problems were solved.

Someone from the audience then asked if the penile implant helped make the husband more romantic? Almost in unison, both ladies on the panel said no, and one lady commented that even though the implant made the erection worth a million bucks, his romantic efforts were still less than two bits in value. This brought a roar of laughter and applause from the audience. However, the point typifies a theme that comes out in our open discussions. With a few guarded exceptions, most of the ladies at the support group meetings agree that their husbands do not give enough attention to romance.

They all stressed that expensive gifts or expensive flowers or an expensive meal or expensive new car are not required to be romantic. When given a survey as to which of the following items most closely correlates with what their husband considers routine foreplay—dinner reservations, surprise bouquet of flowers, surprise new dress, a special thank-you hug for fixing dinner, drawing her a tub of water for her bath, or making a comment like, "Betty Sue, it's time to get in the truck"— most women said "It's time to get in the truck, Betty Sue" came more closely to their husband's idea of foreplay.

Let's just say that represents a rather pitiful testimonial to the romantic efforts and energies of a large number of men. We'll talk more about this in our last chapter, "What's Love Got To Do With It."

Oh, How We Forget Pain

Over the 15 years we've had "Potency Restored" meetings in Montgomery, up until his untimely death two years ago, Reverend Ed Freeman was a significant force in the spirit of this support group. I don't know how many lives he touched and influenced in his ministry, but with his attendance over a thirteen-year period at the support group meetings, he played a major role in the lives of several hundred men and their wives. I'll always remember the time several years ago when he was on the panel at one of our discussion programs when someone asked how much pain he experienced after his penile implant surgery. Without hesitation he said, "Oh, I had no pain at all. There was no pain whatsoever following the surgery. I went home the next day and didn't have to take anything for pain at all."

Of course, almost everybody does take something for pain after surgery and sometimes they come back for the first two or three weeks after penile implant surgery wishing they had not had the surgery because of the degree of discomfort and swelling. But as long as they use a lot of ice packs the first couple of weeks, most men are able to discontinue their pain medicines within a couple of weeks.

The Chase

A couple of years back a 75-year-old gentleman who was then about six months post-penile implant surgery was in attendance and volunteered to participate in the panel discussion that evening. I was a bit surprised he was willing to be that talkative, since he had only had the implant in for about six months. During the discussion, he was asked what his partner thought about his inflatable prosthesis. He broke up the house when he declared, "When I start to pumping, she starts to running."

Plain Talk Summary: Role of Impotence Support Groups — Potency Restored

Impotence support groups such as "Potency Restored" are primarily an educational forum. In addition to the usual lectures, presentations, and academic ways of passing on information, individuals with erectile dysfunction have an opportunity to meet with other individuals and couples who have had this symptom and had the problem treated successfully. In this informal setting, patients have the opportunity to learn specific details from individuals who have undergone surgery or who have tried previous nonsurgical treatment options. A number of these support groups have been in existence since the mid-1980s around the United States. In those instances, the groups all have couples who have participated for greater than ten years, and who provide the solid nucleus of members who are there to help with newly diagnosed individuals and couples who are referred to these free, confidential meetings.

15

P L A N T S   C A N   D O   I T

Herbal Medicines for Males

W hile the natural treatment of many diseases has been documented for centuries, only in the last 20 years have herbal medicines become more popular for the treatment of erectile dysfunction. I am frequently asked by patients if it's okay to take this one or that one and in the past have always told them that as long as the herbal medicine didn't cause any significant side effects, to go ahead and take them. For the most part, the herbal medicines either increase male libido or, in some cases, may play a role in improving arterial circulation. We will look at six widely used natural medicines.

Yohimbine

Yohimbine hydrochloride is a drug that is isolated from the bark of the Yohimbe tree (Pausinystalia Johimbe). This tree is native to tropical west Africa. Yohimbine has no effect whatsoever on testosterone levels. While it does have some impact on libido, causing an increased sex drive in some younger patients, its primary action is to increase arterial blood flow to erectile tissue. Yohimbine has been reported to be successful in up to 40 percent of patients.[148, 149] My own personal experience, and that of many other urologists, would put the effectiveness at less than 5 percent. In some younger patients I have seen Yohimbine work fairly effectively. On the other hand, side effects include anxiety, palpitations, increases in blood pressure, dizziness, headache, and skin flushing. Even though Yohimbine has been approved by the FDA for treating impotence, the Yohimbe bark has not been approved and in fact has been classified by the FDA as an unsafe herb.[150] This concern is because of the variability in the content of Yohimbe in various commercial preparations. Therefore, when using Yohimbine, it's best to use a product from a reputable company that clearly labels the level of Yohimbine per dosage.

Potency Wood (Muira Puama)

Folklore has it that this is one of the best herbs for treating decreased libido. Potency Wood, also known as Muira Puama (Ptychopetalum olacoides), is a shrub native to Brazil, and has long been known to be a powerful aphrodisiac as well as a nerve stimulant, according to South American folk medicine.[151] One recent clinical study has validated its safety and shown effectiveness, as well, in improving libido in some patients.[152] A 1990 clinical study at the Institute of Sexology in Paris, France, demonstrated the effectiveness of Muira Puama extract for males with lack of sexual desire and inability to obtain or maintain an erection. At a dose of 1 to 1.5 grams per day, 62 percent of patients with a loss of libido reported a significantly positive effect. As many as half of the patients with erectile failure felt the Muira Puama was of some benefit. The exact mechanism of action of this herbal medicine is still unknown. Apparently, it works both on the psychological and physical aspects of initiating and maintaining an erection.

Ginkgo Biloba Extract

Extract from Ginkgo biloba has been shown to be beneficial in the treatment of erectile dysfunction due to lack of blood flow.[153] In this particular study, a group of patients were evaluated when they had as a group not reacted or responded positively to papaverine injections (up to 50 mg.). These patients were then treated with Ginkgo biloba extract at 60 mg. per day for 12 to 18 months. With regular monitoring of Doplar ultrasound, in this first study, improved blood flow was noted after six to eight weeks. At six months after initiation of the Ginkgo biloba extract, about 50 percent of the patients had regained some potency. Of those who had not regained potency on simply Ginkgo biloba extract alone, a revisit to the papaverine injection protocol was successful in about 20 percent. Twenty-five percent still had no response with papaverine and the remaining 5 percent showed no change in blood flow by ultrasound. Another study evaluated the effectiveness of Ginkgo biloba extract at a higher dosage, 80 mg. taken three times a day.[154] In this study the patients were divided into groups who either responded previously to an injection protocol with vasoactive drugs or did not respond at all to the injection protocol. Both groups were given the 80 mg. dose three times a day. All of the patients had been suspected of having primarily an arterial insufficiency problem. Those patients in the group who had previously responded to the injection protocol also responded favorably to the Ginkgo biloba extract. In the second group, of the 30 men who were given the Ginkgo extract, 19 responded positively and were able to obtain and maintain an erection with the help of the vasoactive drug injection into the erectile tissue. Eleven in the second group still did not see any response with the injection protocol after taking Ginkgo extract.

Damiana (turnera diffusa)

Damiana leaves have been used in the United States since 1874 as an aphrodisiac. Damiana has been very popular even though there are no clinical studies to support its effectiveness. It is rarely used alone and is typically combined with other herbs in commercial preparations. It may increase sensitivity in the penis by causing a urethral irritation.[151] Therefore, drinking a cup of Damiana tea has been suggested for those individuals who wish to try the its effects. However, they should expect some urethral irritation.

Panax ginseng

Human studies supporting the role of ginseng in restoring sexual function have not supported its effectiveness in animal studies. Ginseng does promote some growth of the testes and does result in increased testosterone levels and increased sexual activity and mating behavior in some animal studies.[155-157] This data supports the use of ginseng for problems with male libido.

The dose of ginseng has been related to the ginsenoside composition. Different products have varying amounts of the different ginsenosides. A typical high quality ginseng root powder or extract might contain 5 percent ginsenosides. In this case the dose would be 100 mg. taken one to three times a day. To avoid side effects, the Russians have recommended, for longterm administration, either Panax ginseng or Siberian ginseng. The recommendation is for use of a therapeutic dose for a period of three weeks followed by a two-week interval without any ginseng at all.

Chaste berry

Chaste berry (Bitex agnus castus) has primarily been used in women to treat premenstrual syndrome and to lower prolactin levels. One study has demonstrated that Chaste berry extract also lowers prolactin levels in men at a dosage of 480 mg. per day. Whether this leads to an improved libido remains to be seen. No clinical trials are available showing it actually increases testosterone or increases libido.

Herbal strategies

The natural approach to erectile dysfunction treatment involves improvements overall in diet, increased regular exercise with avoidance of bad health practices such as smoking or excess alcohol and drug consumption, nutritional supplements with multivitamins, including Vitamin C at doses up to 500 mg. three times a day, Vitamin E at 400-800 IU per day, one tablespoon daily of flaxseed oil, and herbs.

In summary, the herbs utilized for a decreased libido include ginseng root powder or extract at a dose of 100 mg. taken one to three times daily for half the days of the month, with no ginseng taken the other 15 days a month. This helps reduce the incidence of any side effects or toxicity associated with ginseng. Anther choice for treating decreased libido includes Muira puama extract at a dose of 250 mg. three times per day.

For arterial insufficiency, Ginkgo biloba extract (24 percent Ginkgo flavonglycosides) is recommended at a dose of 80 mg. three times a day.

For those men with elevated prolactin levels, Chaste berry (Vitex agnus castus) extract (0.5 percent agnuside) is suggested at a dose of 350-500 mg. daily.

When patients ask my recommendation for a natural herbal medicine for erectile dysfunction, I provide them with the information summarized above. Clinical studies showing dramatic improvements are not available, but yet these particular herbal medicines all meet the first rule of medicine, in that "they first do no harm." I don't think it hurts to try some of these herbal entities either alone or in combination.

Plain Talk Summary: Herbal Medicines for the Treatment of Erectile Dysfunction

Herbal medicines have been evaluated for their role in treating erectile dysfunction, primarily via the mechanisms of improving libido and increasing arterial circulation to the erectile tissue. Several commonly utilized natural extracts are discussed in terms of their potential benefit and the dosage recommended. The best approach when considering natural therapy for treating erectile dysfunction is to combine any or all of these herbal agents with other nutritional supplements such as multivitamins and extra Vitamin C, Vitamin E, and flaxseed oil. Improving one's lifestyle by avoiding the excesses of alcohol consumption, cigarette smoking and illicit drug utilization, combined with a regular exercise program provides a healthier and more fit individual. In fact, studies have shown that those experience an overall greater degree of sexuality enhancement to the degree the individual fitness improved.[158] For example, frequency of intimate activities, reliability of adequate function during sexual intercourse, percentage of satisfactory orgasms, all improved with individuals who improve their physical fitness.[158]

16

E N T E R   V I A G R A !

Viagra for Male Erectile Dysfunction

N o drug has experienced media attention than Pfizer's new oral therapy for erectile dysfunction, Viagra. The television talk show hosts may seem excited about Viagra, but the patients who have actually used Viagra for the last five months are the ones who really have something to talk about. Patients for whom we prescribe Viagra usually have many questions and they tend to be the same questions. Therefore, in this chapter I will outline the material in a question and answer format.

1. How does Viagra work?

Viagra, the citrate salt of sildenafil, is not an aphrodisiac. It is not a hormone. It does not affect sexual drive. Rather, it enhances the blood mechanics which produce an erect penis when the happy owner of the penis is sexually stimulated. You may remember the rather technical explanation in Chapter 1 of the mechanism of erection of the penis. Reviewing that discussion reminds us of the role of nitric oxide (NO) in the corpus cavernosum during sexual stimulation.[14] NO then activates the enzyme guanylate cyclase, which results in increased levels of cyclic guanosine monophosphate (cGMP). The cGMP induces smooth muscle relaxation in the corpus cavernosum [see Figure 5], allowing inflow of blood into the vascular spaces in the corpus cavernosum. Viagra works by enhancing the effect of nitric oxide (NO) by inhibiting phosphodi-esterase 5 (PDE 5), which is responsible for the degradation of cGMP, our hero, in the corpus cavernosum. With sexual stimulation there is the release of local NO. In the patient who has taken Viagra, its inhibition of PDE 5 causes increased levels of cGMP in the corpus cavernosum, resulting in relaxation of the smooth muscles in the erectile tissue and inflow of blood into the corpus cavernosum. Viagra has no effect, therefore, in the absence of sexual stimulation.

Laboratory studies have demonstrated that Viagra is selective for PDE 5. It has been shown to be a thousand-fold more selective for PDE 5 than for PDE 2, PDE 3, and PDE 4. It's important that it has very little selectivity for PDE 3 since that enzyme is involved in the control of heart muscle contractility. On the other hand, Viagra is only about tenfold as selective for PDE 5 as it is for PDE 6, an enzyme bound to the retina. This slight bit of selectivity in laboratory studies for PDE 6 probably is the basis for some reported abnormalities related to color vision in patients taking higher doses, 100 mg. or greater, of Viagra.

About here patients stop me and say, "Wait a minute. Could you put all of what you just said in much simpler terms? How do the Viagra molecules know that they're supposed to go to the penis to tie up the PDE 5 enzyme of that breaking down cGMP?"[159, 160]

At this point I try to use some analogy such as the red Volkswagen story. In that case a bank that was robbed in New York City reported having a large number of red Volkswagen Beetles pull up out front and a number of armed robbers came in and robbed the bank. These robbers escaped the state of New York and there ensued a national hunt for anyone driving red Volkswagen Beetles. The FBI extended their search into every state and monitored all highways and major roads looking for the red Beetles. Once the first and second Beetles were reported outside of Nashville, all of the FBI agents that were searching in the other 49 states moved into Tennessee and began to surround Nashville. The FBI agents had a number to search for and find and apprehend the red Volkswagens. All of the FBI agents then congregated at an antique car show in Nashville. They found the 15 red Volkswagens and their owners, who had participated in the bank robbery. At this point they apprehended the "bad guys," the owners of the red Volkswagens. In the case of Viagra and its role in the body, once Viagra is taken orally it circulates throughout the entire body much like the FBI agents circulated throughout the entire United States. The Viagra molecules have a specific order to bind to only phosphodiesterase 5, or PDE 5, just as the FBI agents had a specific order to apprehend only the drivers of red Volkswagens. Just as occasionally the FBI agents would stop and apprehend another criminal, the Viagra occasionally binds to other phosphodiesterase-type enzymes such as PDE 2, PDE 3, PDE 4, and PDE 6 on occasion. Once the FBI located all of the bank robbers in one location, they apprehended them, tied them up and took them out of commission. This is what happens in the body to the circulating Viagra. Once the Viagra encounters the PDE 5 molecules, which happen to be isolated in the smooth muscle cells of the erectile tissue in the corpus cavernosum, they apprehend and tie up the PDE 5 inside those muscle cells. As we have seen schematically in Figure 5, with PDE 5 out of the way, cGMP is allowed to maintain relaxation of the smooth muscle in the corpus cavernosum and penile arteries for a continued inflow of blood into the erectile tissue and a sustained erection.

2. How fast does the drug work?

Viagra is rapidly absorbed when taken orally. Studies have shown that its maximum observed blood concentrations are reached within 30 minutes to 120 minutes. The average time for maximum blood level is about 60 minutes. Again, the advantage of this pill is that it works very naturally and requires stimulation. If there's no stimulation, there will be no erection. The beneficial effect can be seen as late as eight hours after taking the tablet. On the other hand, most of the effectiveness is reached within the first four hours, therefore the pill should be taken from one to two hours prior to intercourse. The absorption efficiency is reduced if the patient takes in a high fat meal. In that setting, also the time to maximum effect is delayed by about 60 minutes. Therefore, I advise patients that they should take the Viagra then take their partner out for a nice dinner, but not to both dinner and a movie. On the other hand, if they eat a high-fat meal, they probably will have time for a short movie following the high-fat content meal, before the Viagra kicks in.

3. What are the main adverse side effects of Viagra?

In placebo-controlled clinical studies the side effects for Viagra (2.5 percent) was not significantly greater than for a placebo (2.3 percent). The adverse events were generally transient and mild to moderate in nature. When Viagra was taken as recommended on an as-needed basis and flexible-dose, placebo-controlled clinical trials, the following adverse events were reported: mild headache (16 percent), flushing (10 percent), indigestion (7 percent), runny nose (7 percent), transient visual disturbance (blue haze) (3 percent), urinary tract infection (3 percent), diarrhea (3 percent), dizziness (2 percent), and finally a rash (2 percent). Other adverse reactions occurred at a rate of greater than 2 percent, but were equally common in the placebo group: respiratory tract infection, back pain, flu syndrome, and arthralgia. As the dose of Viagra increases up to 100 mg., dyspepsia (indigestion) increased to 17 percent and abnormal vision increased to 11 percent. Viagra did not cause any problems with night vision or blurry vision.

4. Are there any absolute contraindications?

The only contraindication to Viagra therapy is the use of nitrates. Nitrates include sublingual nitroglycerine, long-acting oral nitrates, and nitrate paste. See Table 4 for a summary of some of the more commonly prescribed nitrates. (Nitrates that are commonly found in many foods are not a contraindication for Viagra.) During the initial FDA studies, several patients fainted while using nitrates and Viagra in combination, due to a drop in blood pressure. Some of the patients who fainted reported having serious consequences after the fainting episode. A number of deaths have been reported since Viagra first became available in early April 1998, of patients who supposedly were using Viagra. At last count, in mid-August 1998, some four months post-availability of Viagra, some reports were running as high as 60 patients who had died who may also have taken Viagra. Questions have been raised as to other possible antihypertensive medication that might interfere with Viagra to cause potentially harmful drops in blood pressure. However, at this point it must be stressed that during the FDA studies, more than 4,000 patients were studied and there was no difference in the number of patients with fainting episodes between the two study groups, those taking Viagra and those taking a placebo. In both cases, the numbers were less than 2 percent.

As of June 8, 1998, the FDA had received 16 reports of deaths of men taking Viagra. On the other hand, none of these deaths has been directly attributed to Viagra alone. Again, this raises the flag of caution for those individuals taking nitrates. During nitrate therapy high levels of nitric oxide (NO) are present in circulation. As we've seen from review of the mechanism of Viagra, the administration of Viagra may potentiate the vasodilatory effect of the circulating NO, resulting in potentially serious low blood pressure.[161]

To date, more than two million prescriptions of Viagra have been written. Data from the National Center for Health Statistics indicated the death rate from all causes in men older than 45 years is approximately 1,600 per million per month. The American Heart Association estimates for cardiovascular deaths are 185 to 275 per million per month.[161] Therefore, the expected death in the population of older men taking Viagra would be well above what has been reported to date.

We as urologists, along with all physicians prescribing Viagra, need to inform patients taking cardiac medicine that there is a degree of cardiac risk associated with most forms of exertional activity, including sexual intercourse, and keep this in mind when counseling and treating this group of patients with erectile dysfunction.[161]

5. How often does it work?

The first reports from clinical studies in the United Kingdom and the United States reported success rates of 83 percent[14] and 92 percent.[162] In the first large placebo-controlled study evaluating the results of 10 mg., 25 mg., and 50 mg. of sildenafil (Viagra), the reported success rates

Table 4: Examples of the More Commonly Prescribed Nitrates (not all-inclusive)

DRUG NAME	MANUFACTURER
Nitroglycerin	
Deponit® (transdermal)	Schwarz Pharma, Inc.
Minitran™	3M Pharmaceuticals
Nitrek	Bertek Pharmaceuticals, Inc.
Nitro-bid®	Hoechst Marion Roussel
Nitrodisc	G.D. Searle Company
Nitro-Dur®	Key Pharmaceuticals, Inc.
Nitrogard™	Forest Pharmaceuticals, Inc.
Nitoglyn	Kenwood Laboratories
Nitrolingual Spray®	Rhône-Poulenc Rorer Pharmaceuticals, Inc.
Nitrol® Ointment (Appli-Kit)®	Savage Laboratories
Nitrong	Rhône-Poulenc Rorer Pharmaceuticals, Inc.
Nitro-par	Parmed Pharmaceuticals
Nitrostat®	Parke-Davis
Nitro-Time	Time-Cap Laboratories
Transderm-Nitro®	Novartis Pharmaceuticals Corp.
Isosorbide Mononitrate	
Imdur®	Key Phamaceuticals, Inc.
Ismo®	Wyeth-Ayerst Laboratories
Monoket Tablets	Schwarz Pharma, Inc.
Isosorbide Dinitrate	
Dilatrate®-SR	Schwarz Phara, Inc.
Isordil®	Wyeth-Ayerst Laboratories
Sorbitrate®	Zeneca Pharmaceuticals
Sodium Nitroprusside	
Erythatyl Tetranitrate	
Pentaerythritol Tetranitrate	

were 65 percent, 79 percent, and 89 percent respectively at these three dosages.[163] A number of placebo-controlled studies have been reported since these early studies from 1995 and 1996. Using successful attempts at adequate sexual intercourse as an endpoint, recent studies have shown a success rate of 69 percent of those men taking Viagra, compared with 22 percent of those men taking a placebo tablet.[164]

At this time, there's no question as to the success of Viagra in producing erections. Recent presentations at the American Urological Association annual meeting in late May 1998, suggests that Viagra improved erections in 84 percent of the men taking the 100 mg. dose[165]; in addition, Viagra produced significant improvements in about half of the patients with the most severe cases of erectile dysfunction at the 50 mg. dose and up to 73 percent of those men taking the 100 mg. dose.[166]

6. Gee, Doc, I'm 73 years old. Will Viagra work as well for me as it does the younger patients?

Yes. Another presentation recently asked this question. Results were compared with men over age 65 and men under age 65. In placebo-controlled, double-blind studies, Viagra in doses from 25 mg. to 100 mg. was found to be equally effective in men over age 65 as in those men under age 65.[167]

7. What dose should I use?

Most of the time the recommended starting dose is 50 mg. The dose may be increased to 100 mg. if 50 mg. does not seem to be quite adequate. On the other hand, if the 50 mg. is very successful, then the dose could be reduced down to as low as 25 mg.

8. Can I overdose on the drug?

As the dose increases, the possibility of side effects has been shown to increase. Viagra is now available in the 100 mg. tablets as the largest available unit dose. In the clinical studies, up to eight of those tablets were taken (800 mg.) without any serious side effects. However, I should quickly point out that doses larger than 100 mg. were not shown to be any more effective than the 100 mg. dose.

8. Is there a maximum age limit?

No. Viagra has been tested and found to be safe and effective in men up to age 85 years old.

9. Will Viagra affect my orgasm?

No. Viagra depends on stimulation to be effective, and orgasms are not reduced or enhanced.

10. I had a radical prostatectomy one year ago. What are the chances of Viagra helping me achieve adequate erections?

In a subgroup of post-radical prostatectomy patients who had erectile dysfunction, the placebo-control group showed a 15 percent response while the treatment group showed a 43 percent response rate to Viagra.

11. Will Viagra increase my sex drive (libido)?

No. Viagra has absolutely no effect on libido.

12. Is there any evidence that Viagra causes cancer in any studies, including studies with experimental animals?

No. After extensive testing in animals, as well as clinical studies in humans, no evidence of cancer causing activity has surfaced.

13. Since I've had several episodes of a prolonged erection following injection with one of the vasoactive drugs directly into the penis, do I have to be concerned that Viagra will cause an erection that will not go down (priapism)?

No. There have been no episodes of priapism in any of the clinical studies with Viagra. Viagra, again, does not cause erections without sexual stimulation.

Unlike the injections which can cause increased blood flow to the penis in the absence of sexual stimulation, the mechanism of Viagra is totally different. Therefore, there is no risk for a sustained erection.

14. I don't take any of the nitrates on the list that you provided that I'm looking at, but I do take a blood pressure pill. Is there a problem with the safety of Viagra while I'm on my blood pressure medicines?

All of the clinical studies have demonstrated that Viagra is safe when taken with non-nitrate antihypertensives (high blood pressure medicines), such as the groups of calcium channel blockers, alpha-blockers, beta-blockers, ACE inhibitors, and diuretics. It is still, however, a good idea to check with your primary physician if you're taking any cardiac medicines. It's important to keep in mind that there is a degree of cardiac risk associated with all forms of exercise and exertional-type activity, including sexual intercourse.

15. I'm a forty-year-old with the problem of primary erectile dysfunction (never had a normal erection). Now that Viagra has allowed me to return to normal erectile function, my wife wants to have a child. Is there any problem with Viagra causing ill effects on her or on the baby?

While effects of Viagra on fertility were not specifically studied in previous studies, there have been several pregnancies during the studies with the first 4,500 men. Viagra has not been found to have any effect at all on sperm motility. In experimental animals it has caused no birth defects and has had no effect on fertility, as well. Thus, there's no direct answer to this question. I would recommend you proceed cautiously and be sure that your wife's obstetrician is also aware that you've been taking Viagra.

16. What is the cost of Viagra?

The cost of Viagra is about the same as some of the newer, very potent antibiotics that are taken on a daily basis for severe prostate infections. This ranges from about eight dollars per tablet up to ten or eleven dollars per tablet in the United States. In other countries, I've heard stories about Viagra being sold on the black market for up to sixty to eighty dollars per tablet.

17. Will my insurance company cover my prescription for Viagra?

In the past, most medication plans from insurance companies did cover other drugs used for treating erectile dysfunction, such as the vasoactive drugs for penile injection. When Viagra first became available in early April of 1998, many insurance plans initially covered all prescriptions with a "wait and see what effect Viagra has on the cost of prescriptions for the individual plan." It did not take long for the insurance plan administrators to realize that the cost for most plans was going to be substantial. The response from insurance companies has varied from an absolute rejection of all Viagra coverage to one of covering Viagra cost, provided the prescribing physician writes a letter supporting the medical necessity of the Viagra. The problem with the latter approach is that there are a number of patients who are not diabetic and who are not post-radical prostatectomy, or post some other type of illness or injury where the etiology is clear-cut. In those individuals without a clear-cut etiology, yet individuals who have a physical problem due to their erectile dysfunction complaints, individuals who have been using penile injections as the only means of achieving an adequate erection have often seen their request for insurance coverage of their Viagra fall on deaf ears. Medicare does not have a drug plan as such and has never covered oral prescription medicine. On the other hand, Medicaid historically has had a drug formulary of covered medicines. Medicaid patients are expected to pay a very small co-pay with each prescription. Other drugs such as papaverine or Caverject, which are used to treat erectile dysfunction by their application with penile injections, have never been covered in the past by Medicaid. Whether Medicaid should now cover Viagra or not has been a question that has received a lot of opinions on both sides. Certainly, one could make the argument that indigent patients should have access to the same care as those non-indigent patients, even though the total numbers of purely Medicaid covered males with erectile dysfunction is, I think, much smaller than some of the projections we hear from state Medicaid directors. In my own practice, which covers a cross section of individuals, I see very few purely Medicaid patients. Most of the patients I see with Medicaid are elderly who have a combination of Medicare and Medicaid. So now we have a situation with Viagra where Medicare and Medicaid have not covered the drug and most private insurance drug plans which initially started covering the drug now have placed a lot of restrictions. So where do we go from here? Fortunately, for the short term, the majority of patients can afford to pay for the drug out of pocket. Looking at the cost from a longer term perspective, I see no reason that the insurance plan actuarial staff could not come up with an option for individuals who wish to have coverage for Viagra or any other future erectile dysfunction medication. This plan could be modeled after the plan currently used for childbearing age females, where the insurance does cost more in premiums for "maternity care."

18. So, Doc, what do I need to do next to try to get my insurance company to cover Viagra?

The next thing I would recommend would be for you and other coworkers, along with your employer, to sit down with someone from your insurance company and tell them what type of coverage you would like. That way the insurance plan actuarial staff can run their numbers on the computer and see what additional premium would be required. Options then might include adding a small amount to the premium for everyone versus increasing the premium just for those males who would like to have "erectile dysfunction coverage," much like childbearing age group females have to pay extra for maternity coverage.

19. Will taking Viagra make me more aggressive, and make me want to get up off the sofa and not be a couch potato, and do things such as wash the dishes and take out the trash?

Unfortunately, no. Previous psychological testing has demonstrated no increase in aggressive behavior or increased libido in men on Viagra.

On the other hand, if one were to do more to be helpful around the house, such as washing dishes, spending less time crashed on the sofa watching TV sports, and taking out the trash before being asked to do so, this no doubt would enhance the patient's relationship with his partner, and along with Viagra allow for a much more satisfactory relationship. For more discussion on this subject of romance, please see Chapter 24.

20. Has Viagra coverage by some insurance companies influenced their coverage for prescription contraceptives?

Yes. Included in the recently passed Federal budget agreement, Federal employee health insurance plans will cover prescription contraceptives if they pay for other drugs. Women's rights groups have praised this change, feeling it was a big step toward the ultimate goal of requiring all private health insurers to cover the costs of birth control pills, diaphragms, and other federally approved contraceptives.

17

UNDER INVESTIGATION

Viagra in Combination
with Injections, VEDs

Almost all possible combinations of treatment of erectile dysfunction have been evaluated. For example, combinations of penile injections with the vacuum erection devices (VEDs) have been studied. In addition, the urethral suppository, MUSE, has been studied in combination with VEDs. All of us who treat large numbers of men with erectile dysfunction have anecdotal cases where we can describe patients who have indeed used a combination of Viagra with close supervision with one of the injections. This is usually done in a patient who is not having a satisfactory response with the penile injection protocol who also does not have a satisfactory response with Viagra. In those individuals, sometimes we are able to see an enhancement with a combination of the two treatment forms, but these combinations should not be done without the close supervision of the patient's urologist. It needs to be stressed again that no clinical studies have been done to evaluate the safety of this approach and until such studies are available, these combinations should be avoided. Studies are ongoing across the country to assess some of these combinations in terms of safety and effectiveness, and within the next year or so we should have an answer to the question of treatment combinations.

18

RESEARCH CONTINUES

Viagra in Combination
with Penile Implants

E ven though penile implants have an excellent track record, with a very high satisfaction rate, patients still ask for some areas of improvement. The major areas of concern are lack of engorgement of the glans penis (the head of the penis), delayed sensation of the glans penis with or without difficulty in achieving orgasm, decreased penile length and less penile girth (width) compared with the natural erection. In Figure 10 we see a comparison of the flaccid and erect state in both the natural erection and in the patient with the inflatable penile prosthesis. In that figure, the main point to be demonstrated is that with the penile implant cylinders inside each corpus cavernosum, the corpus cavernosum erectile tissue is still present but is compressed by the inflated cylinders. The amount of erectile tissue available to respond to stimuli and allow blood flow into the penis at times of sexual stimulation is usually a minor amount of capacity. In fact, only about 2 to 3 percent of the patients state they can have some natural penile erection activity while the penile prosthesis cylinders are in the flaccid state. The other point to be made from the diagram is that with the cylinders inflated, there is no increase in girth and engorgement of the corpus spongiosum. With the natural erection, the corpus spongiosum does increase in girth, allowing for engorgement of the glans penis. Since the corpus cavernosum

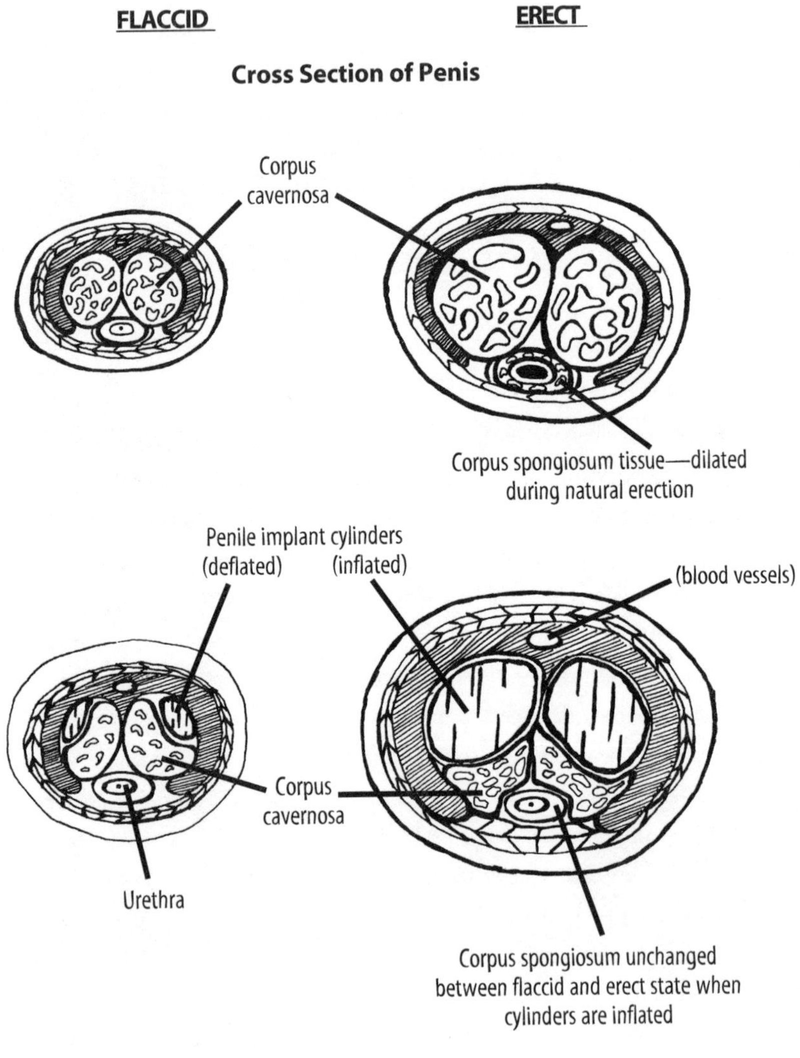

FLACCID   ERECT

Cross Section of Penis

Corpus cavernosa

Corpus spongiosum tissue—dilated during natural erection

Penile implant cylinders
(deflated)   (inflated)

(blood vessels)

Corpus cavernosa

Urethra

Corpus spongiosum unchanged between flaccid and erect state when cylinders are inflated

Fig. 10: Inflatable Penile Implants, Cross-section View

cylinders extend out into the glans penis, therefore the inflatable cylinders also extend into the glans penis. So there is some rigidity to the glans due to the natural anatomical location of these inflatable cylinders about midway into the glans penis. On the other hand, the glans is not engorged with warm, body temperature blood as is the case in a natural erection. So, the lack of extra blood flow no doubt contributes to a decrease in sensation in the patient with an erection from an inflatable prosthesis versus a natural erection.

The question has been asked: "Could Viagra increase circulation to the corpus spongiosum and thereby increase the engorgement of the glans penis?" Also, "Could Viagra allow some patients to have warm blood flowing into the corpus spongiosum tissue as well as the corpus cavernosum to the extent that the inflatable penile cylinders would not have to be pumped up to their usual inflated diameter?" Other questions include: "If Viagra did improve glans penis engorgement, would the patients see an improvement in sensation and a decrease in the sometimes prolonged time to orgasm that some post-implant patients report?"

These and other questions can be addressed in a double-blind, placebo-controlled study comparing Viagra to placebo in men who have an inflatable penile implant in place. Such a study is currently underway in my practice, and probably in other urology clinics across the country.

19

WHAT NEXT?

Future Treatment Developments for Male Erectile Dysfunction

Over the past few decades, as we have seen, there have been a number of exciting developments for the treatment of male sexual dysfunction, especially erectile dysfunction. From the injectable vaso-active drugs, to the semi-rigid and inflatable penile prostheses, to the recent groundbreaking introduction of Viagra, these developments have steadily advanced the ability of health care professionals to help couples achieve satisfying sexual relations. Research continues, of course, and more new developments can be expected. Some of the most-needed research is now being directed to the area of female sexual dysfunction.

New Oral Drugs

Over the last few years, oral phentolamine (Vasomax) has been shown to be effective for men with erectile dysfunction in two small series of patients.[168, 169] A more recent report on the effectiveness and safety of oral Vasomax, presented by Dr. Irwin Goldstein at the annual American Urological Association meeting in May 1998, reviewed the results of a large group of patients evaluated in the Vasomax study group.[170] Review of the placebo-controlled results with both the 40-mg. and 80-mg. dose of phentolamine highlighted the fact that phentolamine is both safe and effective. For patients with mild to moderate erectile dysfunction, the 80 mg. dose was found to improve erectile function in 45 percent of 159 patients, compared with only 16 percent of the placebo group reporting an improvement. Phentolamine is an alpha-adrenoceptor antagonist that blocks the actions of epinephrine and norepinephrine. By reducing the sympathetic nerve tone, Vasomax relaxes both arterial and corpus cavernosum smooth muscle. This results in an increased flow of blood into the sinusoidal and lacunar spaces of the corpus cavernosum, the cylinders. As the trabecular smooth muscle dilates and fills with blood, it compresses the small subtunical veins as discussed in Chapter 1.[171] Both Viagra and Vasomax, working by different mechanisms, result in removal of calcium from smooth muscle cells. While Viagra works inside the smooth muscle cell, where it binds to PDE 5, phentolamine binds to receptors on the surface of the smooth muscle cell. Phentolamine has onset of action to produce its effects in about 20 minutes, compared with Viagra's 30 to 60 minutes for onset of effects. In addition, since phentolamine blocks both alpha 1 and alpha 2 adrenergic receptors, there are less vascular side effects compared with other alpha blocking agents such as Yohimbine, which blocks only one receptor, according to Dr. Goldstein.[170] Like Viagra, phentolamine does not produce increased libido or act as an aphrodisiac. Like Viagra, it does not produce erections, but allows for better blood flow into the penis and better erections in response to stimulation. Another feature of phentolamine is that it does not interact with nitrates. In the most recently reported large series of patients[170] there were no serious adverse events. The side effects with the 40 mg. phentolamine dose occurred in less than 10 percent of the patients and included headaches, facial flushing and some nasal congestion. With the larger 80 mg. dose, increases in the incidents of dizziness, increased heart rate (tachycardia), and small changes in blood pressure have been reported, but in less than 5 percent of the patients, except for tachycardia. In summary, once the FDA gives final approval for widespread use of phentolamine (Vasomax), it will have an application for patients with mild to moderate levels of erectile dysfunction, especially those patients who currently are taking nitrates.

Apomorphine has been shown in a small series of patients, particularly patients with psychogenic erectile dysfunction or mild organic disease, to result in erectile response. Its mechanism of action is thought to primarily be through a central dopamine receptor effect in the brain. Until recently, only several small series of patients with either psychogenic or unknown causes to their erectile dysfunction have been reported to have success with sublingual (taken below the tongue) apomorphine.[172, 173] In a small series, patients with diabetes also were found to have some response to apomorphine.[174] A larger study for this dopaminergic agent was recently reported.[175] A multi-center, double-blind study of 457 patients with erectile dysfunction without any major organic component were randomized to either 2 mg., 4 mg., 6 mg. of apomorphine SL (sublingual) and the placebo. The percentage of attempts resulting in an erection firm enough for intercourse was greater than a placebo in each of the three groups: 46 percent for 2 mg. vs 32 percent for placebo, 52 percent for 4 mg. vs 35 percent for placebo, and 60 percent for 6 mg. vs 34 percent for a placebo. The most common side effect was nausea, usually mild to moderate at an incidence of 39 percent, 19 percent and 2 percent for patients taking 6-mg., 4-mg., and 2-mg. doses respectively. The placebo incidence was at 4.9 percent. Of that 6 mg. group who had the greatest experience with nausea, only 2.7 percent reported severe nausea. There was no severe nausea in lower doses. Therefore, this centrally acting oral drug is effective and is well-tolerated for erectile dysfunction in patients with no major physical component. Sublingual apomorphine, like oral phentolamine, has a very rapid rate of absorption, and therefore onset of action within 20 to 30 minutes.

Other Treatments for Male Erectile Dysfunction

Currently, research efforts are also underway evaluating several new topical agents that could be used in a patch or surface application to the penis. In addition, studies of combinations of two different oral agents or oral and injectable are underway for application to the more difficult erectile dysfunction cases.

At the molecular level, several laboratories are currently making progress in the understanding of the biochemistry of the smooth muscle in the corpus cavernosum tissue.[176]

For treatment of the most severe form of curvature associated with Peyronie's disease, Lue and associates recently reported a 96 percent success rate with a large series of patients, using the technique of incising the Peyronie's plaque and grafting with a venous patch, usually from the saphenous vein.[177] At the other end of the spectrum, for patients with Peyronie's disease in the early, painful phase of the inflammatory process, Iontophoresis, a noninvasive method to enhance transdermal drug transport, has recently been reported.[178] Down the road, the results of current molecular level research, may lead to the application of gene therapy for both the prevention and treatment of the problem of male erectile dysfunction. Do not expect any clinical applications any time soon with gene therapy.

20

A LOT TO LEARN

Understanding Normal
Female Sexual Function

Our understanding of the basic physiology of female sexual function is many years behind where we are with our under standing of male sexual function. Most of the research to date has been done in this area by psychiatrists. In part, this may explain why many of the problems with female sexual dysfunction that are encountered are felt to be of psychological etiology. Where female sexual dysfunction is concerned, it is as if we were in the early 1970s and talking about male erectile dysfunction. As our understanding of basic physiology of the male erection has improved, we now realize that the vast majority of problems with male erectile dysfunction are based on physical rather than psychological causes. Fortunately, for females the tide is turning away from considering any discussion of sexual function or sexual dysfunction as a taboo. As our basic understanding of the biology of the key components of female sexual function progresses, and more drugs are developed to impact and treat these basic biological mechanisms, physicians will change their attitude as they have changed their approach to treating male erectile dysfunction. Whereas, thirty years ago, whenever a male patient over the age of 60 would ask his primary care physician about something to take for his erectile dysfunction problem, the answer he often got from his physician was similar to, "Well, Charlie, at your age why don't you just do more fishing and hunting and take up some other hobbies?"

The purpose of this chapter is to review the biology of major components of female sexual function. The major areas to be discussed include sexual desire (or libido), arousal, and orgasm.[179]

Sexual Desire

Early studies looking at female sexual desire focused on the role of the reproductive hormones in healthy adult women during different phases of the menstrual cycle.[180] These studies found peaks of sexual desire during virtually every phase of the menstrual cycle. The pre- and post-menstrual phases have been most frequently identified [180] Other factors, such as cyclic changes in mood and energy, no doubt have influenced menstrual cycle variations in female libido.[181] Another study involving normally cyclic women found that increased sexual interest during a particular phase of the menstrual cycle was influenced by enhanced well-being during this particular phase.

Problems in finding reliable conclusions regarding sexual desire from menstrual cycle research directed research efforts toward evaluation of individual steroids. Most studies have focused on testosterone with the assumption that it is the "libido-enhancing hormone" in women.[179] This concept was derived initially from anecdotal, uncontrolled observations of female patients who previously had their ovaries removed and adrenal glands removed for malignancy, or those females who were treated with androgens for gynecologic disorders.[182] However, measurements of circulating testosterone relative to measures of sexual desire in normal women have proven inconsistent. On the one hand, one study found that mid-cycle testosterone levels were correlated with intercourse frequency.[183] Meanwhile,[184] another study found that testosterone levels correlated with measures of sexual interest in adolescent girls, but the important factor was peer group relations in determining the onset of coital experiences. These and other studies[185] have demonstrated the difficulty in characterizing sexual desire. No doubt, a combination of hormonal effects, psychosocial events, and the individual female's personality characteristics interact to result in an individual's sexual expression.

Several studies have shown sexual desire in young women to be independent of variations of estradiol and progesterone levels.[186, 187] On the other hand, there is some evidence that sexual desire declines following removal of the ovaries (oophorectomy) in premenopausal women, and that this sexual desire may be restored with either estrodial or a combination of testosterone and estrodial.[188]

In post-menopausal women, estrogen deficiency is primarily responsible for the decrease in pelvic vasocongestion, atrophy of the vaginal epithelium (lining surface), and decreased vaginal lubrication. Estrogen replacement therapy can fully restore adequate vaginal function. In fact, controlled hormone replacement studies demonstrated that adding androgen (testosterone) to an estrogen replacement regimen resulted in enhancement of sexual desire and enjoyment in post-menopausal women.[188] At the same time, vaginal muscle function studies have provided inconsistent evidence of testosterone effects on vasocongestive responses during sexual arousal. Therefore, it appears that in women, as we saw earlier in men, androgens (testosterone) are more important for sustaining sexual desire than for producing any specific physiologic response.

Sexual Arousal

The second stage of female sexual response is arousal. This stage is characterized by a subjective sense of sexual excitement and pleasure, secondary to both physical and emotional stimulation. This stimulation may lead to breast and genital vasodilation and clitoral engorgement. In the female, dilation and engorgement of the blood vessles in the labia and the tissue surrounding the vagina produce what has been called the "orgasmic platform." This is an area at the distal third of the vagina where blood becomes sequestered. Localized perivaginal swelling and vaginal lubrication make up the first changes in this stage of sexual response. This is followed by a ballooning of the proximal portion of the vagina, along with elevation of the uterus.

The relationship between menstrual cycle hormonal variations and sexual arousability has been studied.[189] For the most part, these studies have failed to identify menstrual cycle-related fluctuations in physiologic arousal.[190] More research is needed with newer methodologies to adequately evaluate the role of hormones on female sexual arousal. Since this area of sexual response in the female consists of increased blood flow to the clitoris and vagina, the analogy is obvious to the increased blood flow into the penis, mediated by nitric oxide (NO) with subsequent penile smooth muscle relaxation resulting in vasodilation of the arteries and sinusoidal spaces in the erectile tissue resulting in occlusion of the venous outflow channels and producing an erection.

The question immediately comes to mind: As Viagra facilitates the nitric oxide mechanism in the male penile erectile tissue, will it do the same thing for the female with resultant increased vaginal engorgement, increased vaginal secretions, and increased clitoral engorgement? Recent reports from laboratory studies, actually looking at the regulatory mechanism of clitoral, cavernosal, and vaginal smooth muscle contractility in rabbits, may shed a lot of light on the above question.[191] In the recent report, contraction of clitoral cavernosal and vaginal smooth muscle was found to be regulated by adronergic nerves. Further, the relaxation of clitoral cavernosal smooth muscle appeared to be regulated primarily by the NO pathway, although other pathways were identified that may require further characterization. From the same research lab in Boston, an additional recent report on the morphological/biochemical characterization of human corpus clitoral smooth muscle cells was reported.[192] From this work, human clitoral smooth muscle cells in culture were found to retain their structural and functional integrity, as well as express a number of functional receptors and PDE 5. Both of these studies support the undertaking of a trial of Viagra in female patients to assess its safety and usefulness in improving female sexual arousal. More importantly, the question then becomes: if Viagra will improve the sexual arousal phase for females as it improves erections for males, will the net result be an improvement in female orgasms? Hopefully, we will have the answer to these questions within the next year or so.

Orgasm

Orgasm is characterized in both sexes by an accumulation and peak of sexual pleasure associated with rhythmic contraction of perineal and reproductive organ structures, cardiovascular and respiratory changes, and the release of sexual tension. There is a large body of information on male orgasmic physiology, focusing on the emission phase, thought to be under thoracolumbar nerve control and mediated by the release of norepinephrine, which acts on alpha adrenergic receptors, the smooth muscles of the seminal vessels, prostate and vas deferens, and propels seminal fluid into the bulbous urethra. A sacral spinal reflex produces the ejaculatory phase in which the striated muscles that surround the bulbous urethra contract rapidly, resulting in the outward projection of semen.[193] In contrast to male orgasmic physiology, little information is available today on the physiology of the female orgasm. Major questions remain to be answered, including, why do women lack a post-orgasmic refractory period? Unlike men, women can experience multiple orgasms. In addition, there's no established answer to the question concerning the difference between a vaginally stimulated orgasm and a clitorally stimulated orgasm. There's still controversay concerning whether different physiological processes underlie these two different types of orgasms.

Although it is felt that the progression from sexual arousal to orgasm is the consequence of a synergistic interaction between genital and psychological stimulation, in some situations cognitive (or central) arousal alone may initiate an orgasmic response. A recent review[194] found that central arousal alone may trigger an orgasm in normal females in response to fantasy, hypnosis, or REM sleep, and even in paraplegic patients.

The extent to which central neurophysiological events are related to both the nature and intensity of orgasmic experiences, and even to the male-female differences in the refractory period, is still unknown. Similarly, there is conflicting evidence regarding the relationship between subjective orgasmic intensity, satisfaction, and duration and peripheral physiologic perameters such as blood pressure, respiratory rate, and heart rate.

The possible functional significance of oxytocin release during arousal and orgasm recently gained attention.[195] In this report, neuroendocrine investigations revealed a link between oxytocin, a neuropeptide hormone, and sexual arousal and orgasm. A positive relationship was found to exist between psychophysiologically measured pelvic musle contractions, blood pressure elevations, and blood increases in oxytocin during orgasm in both men and women. In addition, in multiorgasmic women, the amount of oxytocin increase correlated well with subjective ratings of the orgasmic intensity.

21

NOT JUST A MAN THING

Female Sexual Dysfunction —
Causes and Treatment

S exual dysfunctions are very common in women.[196] In a recent review of 329 healthy women seen in an outpatient gynecologic clinic,[197] 58 percent reported significant orgasm difficulties, 38 percent complained of anxiety or inhibition during sex, 28 percent were no longer sexually active, and 18 percent of the women complained of frequent pain with intercourse. In this same study, 68 percent of the women reported being somewhat to very satisfied with their overall sexual relationship despite the reported sexual dysfunction difficulties. This finding that sexual relationship satisfaction is not exclusively determined by sexual functioning had previously been emphasized in an earlier report of happily married women who reported a rather high rate of sexual dysfunction (63 percent).[198] These studies demonstrate that women can and do tolerate a certain level of sexual dysfunction before considering it a problem or reporting any type of marital dissatisfaction.

Until recently, most of the research studies and reports on female sexual dysfunction have been carried out by psychiatrists and psychologists. As was the case with male sexual dysfunction 25 years ago, most problems with females have been considered to be psychological in origin. This fact, combined with a hesitancy on the part of the patient and health care providers to bring up the subject of female sexual dysfunction, has contributed to a lack of attention to this important clinical area. Other factors such as limited research funds have added to the shortage of basic science information about female sexual function. On a positive note, more attention has been turned recently to female problems in the basic science laboratories. Some of those same investigators who have done an excellent job of pushing back the frontier of basic science regarding male sexual function have now turned their attention to female sexual function and female sexual dysfunction. Thus, urologists, who previously had focused primarily on male sexual dysfunction problems, are now leading the way in basic laboratory research to better understand all components of female sexual function. This will soon lead to new medical treatments for female problems, based on a better understanding of the biology of smooth muscle function in the vaginal wall, for example. With time, most of the problems with female sexual function that we will discuss in this chapter may ultimately be found to have physical rather than primarily psychological causes.

In this chapter we will touch on a number of lifespan experiences for women and their impact on women's sexuality, including menstrual cycles, pregnancy, menopause, hysterectomy, drug influences, and the influence of pelvic and breast malignancies. We will also look at current approaches to diagnosing and treating disorders of libido, sexual arousal, orgasm, and disorders of sexual pain.

One classic way to try to categorize female sexual dysfunction has been to divide it into physical versus psychological versus interactional factors. While all these factors play a role in determining female sexual response and are all very important, there's so much overlap between physical and psychological and between psychological and interactional that it's difficult to isolate one component. There are a few isolated factors in each category.

Physical Factors

Normal vascular and nerve supply to the pelvis, along with absence of depression and anxiety, are essential for adequate sexual function. Anything that interferes with circulation to the pelvis or impairs nerve function can cause problems. For example, a number of specific bio-chemical entities interfere with libido and response. These include *decreased* alpha adrenergic and cholinergic activity, dopamine, leutinizing hormone-releasing hormone, androgens, and *increased* serotonin, corti-sol, and progesterone.[199] Any condition or medication that impacts the level of these chemicals may impair sexual response. Nerve damage caused by illnesses, such as multiple sclerosis or peripheral neuropathy caused by chronic alcohol abuse, may impact sensation and orgasmic capacity. In addition, drugs such as heroin or methadone decrease physical sexual arousal. Cocaine and amphetamines may initially en-hance libido and arousal, while ultimately delaying or inhibiting orgasm. One who uses cocaine and amphetamines over a longer period of time will experience a decrease in sexual satisfaction.

Psychological Factors

Acute or chronic stress as indicated by symptoms of fatigue and sleep disturbance is the most common psychological factor. Stress symptoms often sound similar to depression symptoms. Gender identity, sexual identity, sexual knowledge and attitudes, and negative body image make up other important psychological factors. Aging, certain illnesses, surgi-cal scarring, and body weight are conditions that often contribute in a negative way to body self-image.

Interactional Factors

A recent or remote history with family or intimate individuals appears to impact partner selection. A woman who has been sexually abused as a child, for example, may choose a partner who seems safe and reliable but not very interested in sex. Interactional factors that often can influence sexual function include: child or adult physical or sexual abuse, attachment issues and sexual patterns and prior relationships, current relationship quality, and commitment. No individual pattern appears to indicate the manner in which earlier experiences predict future function-ing. When earlier sexual experiences are linked to frightening, manipu-lative, painful, taboo, or degrading emotional experiences, they will contribute to later sexual attraction and avoidance patterns. Usually, the culmination of physical, psychological, and interactional factors is the rule rather than the exception.

Diagnosis and Treatment of Sexual Dysfunction in Females

The American Psychiatric Association currently classifies female sexual dysfunction into the categories shown in Table 5. The American Psychiatric Association's *Diagnostic and Statistical Manual,* fourth edition (DSM-IV), uses this as a guide for a clinical assessment.[200] There are, for practical purposes, four areas of disorders. The first four categories included in Table 5 will be discussed individually. When obtaining a history from the patient, it's important to modify each category by whether the disorder is lifelong and whether it's generalized or situational. A complete history includes asking the patient about each of the basic categories. The symptoms must be accompanied by significant distress or interpersonal difficulty to qualify as a disorder in the DSM-IV.

Sexual Desire Disorders

By far, the largest single reason for decreased female libido is lack of satisfaction with their mate's behavior. The offending behavior can range from physical abuse to inattention. This symptom of a troubled relationship is often very difficult to treat. It's important to keep in mind that a depressed sex drive by itself is almost never the sole manifestation of other diseases.

Another very common reason for decreased libido is depression. Again, a careful history will usually show that a depressed sex drive is almost never the only symptom of depression. When the history suggests that depression is the likely cause of a decreased libido, psychiatric consultation is usually the most appropriate treatment approach. Other important physical factors impacting sexual desire are general health, hormonal status and use of both prescription and recreational drugs. Medications reported to decrease sexual interest include a number of antidepressants and certain anti-psychotics.[201] Individual drugs that have been shown to decrease libido include: Cimetidine, Clomipramine,

Table 5: Female Sexual Dysfunctions

Sexual desire disorders

Hypoactive sexual desire disorder: persistent or recurrent absence or deficit of sexual fantasies and desire for sexual activity; take into account factors that affect sexual functioning such as age, sex, life context; rule out other psychiatric disorders such as major depression anxiety.

Sexual aversion disorder: persistent or recurrent aversion to and avoidance of genital contact with a sexual partner; rule out other psychiatric disorders such as major depression, anxiety or obsessive-compulsive disorder.

Sexual arousal disorder

Partial or total lack of physical response as indicated by lack of lubrication and vasocongestion of genitals.

Orgasmic disorder

Persistent delay or absence of orgasm. Lack of coital orgasm is usually considered a normal variation of female sexual response if the woman is able to experience orgasm with a partner using other, noncoital methods. Take sexual experience into account.

Sexual pain disorders

Dyspareunia: recurrent genital pain before, during, or after intercourse; rule out physical disorder, vaginismus and lack of lubrication.

Vaginismus: recurrent involuntary spasm of the outer third of the vagina interfering with or preventing coitus; rule out physical disorder or other psychiatric disorder (rare).

Sexual dysfunctions not otherwise specified

Examples: anesthesia with arousal and orgasm; genital pain during noncoital activities; lack of pleasure during sex.

Fenfluramine, Methazolamide, Methyldopa, Propranolol, Reserpine, Spironolactone, Timolol, and Lithium.[202] Other factors that often impair sexual desire include: sudden events such as loss of a family member or loss of a job, cumulative factors such as the psychological response to aging, life milestones such as children leaving home, and ongoing chronic relationship distress.

Treatment of women with clear androgen deficiencies—for example, those produced by surgical removal of both ovaries or chemotherapy—often is enhanced by the administration of low doses of testosterone.[203] While the use of testosterone has been shown to increase desire, its use in large doses should be viewed with caution in longterm intervention because of the potential cardiovascular side effects. When decreased libido is not due to a physical disorder, an individual may be treated with psychotherapy.[204] However, decreased sexual desire is one of the more difficult sexual disorders to treat. Psychotherapy, often requiring 15 to 45 sessions, has a success rate well under 50 percent.[204] What is needed is a safe, effective oral agent for improving female libido, which works by a mechanism other than hormonal.

Sexual Arousal Disorders

As we saw in Chapter 20, sexual arousal is characterized by a sense of sexual excitement and pleasure accompanied in the male by penile tumescence and in the female by pelvic vasocongestion, vaginal lubrication, and swelling of the external genitalia. Very little physiologic research has been dedicated to understanding the basic mechanisms involved in female sexual arousal compared to male erectile function. No doubt, a normal vascular and neurologic system leading to the vaginal wall and pelvis is required. One would expect, for example, that patients with vascular disease—for example, those females with a long history of cigarette smoking—would manifest problems just as the male has problems with penile tumescence when there is a history of smoking. Clinically, complaints of difficulty lubricating have been the primary singular disorder associated with sexual arousal. This accounts for 18 to 22 percent of the female sexual dysfunction complaints according to one review.[196] Sometimes problems with sexual arousal are associated with simultaneous problems with dyspareunia, or difficulty achieving orgasm. In addition, a lack of lubrication may lead to discomfort with intercource which subsequently impairs subjective arousal. When the woman's partner interprets lack of lubrication to mean lack of interest, this can result in a significant stress in the sexual relationship.

Very little data is available in delivering the treatment for sexual arousal disorders since the condition is considered rare in the absense of pain or orgasmic dysfunction. Currently, for women who have vaginal dryness or difficulty lubricating, the recommendation is for topical lubricants such as K-Y Jelly (Johnson and Johnson), Astroglide (Biofilm), Replense (Parke-Davis), or estrogenic compounds. Recommending estrogenic topical lubricants depends on the woman's physical condition and her risk factors for estrogen therapy. Since this phase of sexual function is analagous to the penile tumescence phase in the male, the question now is: Will Viagra help these females with arousal difficulty by improving blood flow to the vaginal wall and therefore improving lubrication and lessening pain with intercourse? We should have the answer to that question within the next year as clinical trials are currently underway at Boston University and other medical centers to assess the safety and effectiveness of Viagra in females.

Orgasmic Disorders

These disorders, as we have seen, are quite common, with 58 percent of women in one study[197] complaining of orgasmic problems. Approximately 10 percent of the women reported global, lifelong lack of orgasm. The remaining 48 percent of the women in that study reported situational or intermittent orgasmic problems. Some classes of medications frequently contribute to problems with orgasm. These include most antidepressants and some antipsychotic drugs (such as Trifluoperazine and Thioridazine). Those patients with lifelong problems with orgasm rarely have a physical underlying etiology. They are best treated with traditional sex therapy techniques. There are a number of books available dealing with self-observation, relaxation, body image, tolerance of sexual arousal tension, acceptance of sexual feelings, and sensual touching that may be used alone or with a partner.[205] If progress is not made using some techniques described in these books, the patient should be evaluated by a sex therapy consultation. Success is generally as high as 75 percent in individuals; however, often up to 20 therapy sessions are required.

The majority of females with problems with orgasm describe their difficulty as situational or intermittent. For these individuals, orgasm problems are more likely to be related to relationship problems and will therefore require additional therapy. At this time we have no medicines for the treatment of orgasm disorders.

Sexual Pain Disorders

• *Dyspareunia.* Dyspareunia is defined as recurrent genital pain before, during, or after intercourse. Its diagnosis requires a careful medical and sexual history, as well as a careful physical examination to identify the type of pain. Up to 18 percent of women in one recent survey of 329 healthy women (age 18 to 73) reported pain frequently with intercourse.[197] Sometimes females have pain at the vaginal entrance, usually caused by local irritation secondary to spermicides or local skin irritation from a yeast infection. This is to be distinguished from deep dyspareunia. Most of the time the most common reason for the deep dyspareunia is that the patient is not fully aroused prior to the penile insertion. The first sign of female sexual arousal, as we recall, is profuse vaginal lubrication. The next sign is expansion of the inner third of the vagina. If the penis is inserted too early in the cycle of female sexual arousal (as unfortunately it often is), a great deal of discomfort will be experienced as the vaginal walls are forcefully separated. This is easily seen as a symptom of a problem the female is experiencing, but the underlying problem again goes back to the male not taking time to prolong foreplay and allow for adequate female sexual arousal. Interestingly, this etiology for dyspareunia can be excluded in those situations where the female is able to continue sexual intercourse to the point that she has an orgasm.

Pelvic masses such as uterine fibroids and also endometriosis can cause dyspareunia. A pelvic mass is frequently obvious on physical exam. Endometriosis, which can cause a lot of localized tenderness, on exam by the physician, similar to what the patient experiences during intercourse, should not be diagnosed without laparoscopic confirmation by the patient's gynecologist. As a urologist, I see many women with chronic dyspareunia secondary to chronic bladder, bladder neck and urethral inflammation that we commonly label as the female urethral syndrome. This also is usually found on physical exam as an area of tenderness in the vaginal wall, on the top part of the vaginal wall where the bladder joins the urethra, a couple of inches inside the vaginal opening. This source of tenderness and pain can be diagnosed and treated by the urologist with a high success rate. Another common cause is low vaginal estrogen levels that cause and aggravate vaginal dryness that results in painful intercourse.

• **Vulvodynia.** Vulvodynia is a syndrome of unexplained vulvar pain, sexual dysfunction, and psychological disability. [206, 207] The incidence of this condition is not known. One recent report suggested that the prevalence of vulvodynia was as high as 15 percent when actively looked for in a gynecology practive. [208] Due to the lack of abnormal physical findings, many of these women have been told over the years that their problem is mainly psychological. Although the onset may be acute, vulvodynia may become a chronic disorder, often following episodes of vaginitis, antimicrobial therapy or other procedures, such as cryosurgery or laser surgery. The pain is usually described as burning, stinging, irritation, or rawness.[205] Most patients with vulvodynia have visited many physicians seeking help, and have tried multiple topical or systemic prescriptions. The age distribution for this problem is highly variable, ranging from mid-twenties to late sixties. A medical history is usually unremarkable. A few patients have a history of sexually transmitted disease.

The pain is typically located in the vulvar vestibulum, which is the inner portion of the vulva. This extends from the mucocutaneous line (where the skin joins the mucosa of the vagina) on the labia manora inward to the hymenal ring where the vaginal mucus membrane begins.

The urethral meatus, along with Skene's glands, Bartholin's glands, and the minor vestibular glands are all located in the vulvar vestibulum.[209, 210] Although examination may visually show no surface changes, pain can be easily elicited by a single swab test, touching the vulvar vestibulum with a moist cotton tip swab, which elicits a sharp pain.

There are several subsets of vulvodynia, but the most prevelent is vulvar vestibulitis syndrome (VVS). This has also been referred to as adenitis, vestibular adenitis, or focal vulvitis. This is the most common subtype of vulvodynia characterized by dyspareunia, severe point tenderness by the swab test, and vestibular inflammation and redness. With severe VVS, dyspareunia totally prohibits sexual intercouse. Although the syndrome was first described over 100 years ago, its cause still remains obscure. While earlier studies tried to link vulvar vestibulitis syndrome to human papilloma virus infection (HPV), the causative link between HPV and VVS has not been demonstrated.

Treatment of VVS has been individualized. Classic VVS can persist unchanged for months or years. Occasionally spontaneous remissions occur. Couseling and education does help the patient to cope with the problem. In the past, those patients with severe incapacitation from vulvar vestibulitis syndrome, up to 60 to 75 percent, benefited from vestibulectomy in which the hymen and the vulvastibulum are surgically excised. However, this should be reserved for the most severe cases and considered only a last resort type procedure.[211, 212]

On a positive note for females with vulvovaginal pain, Glazer and associates have used a new type of instrumentation, surface electromyography (sEMG), a specific type of biofeedback, in the treatment of vulvodynia and vulvar vestibulitis.[213] Not only did the study demonstrate effectivness in treating the pain associated with vulvodynia, but valuable information was gained regarding the role of pelvic floor muscle stability. The researchers wanted to determine which characteristics of the pelvic floor muscle were associated with pain relief. They discovered that the stability of the muscle at rest was the only characteristic that predicted pain relief. Using this technique in a similar fashion for treating incontinent patients, the goal is to increase control by strengthening the pelvic floor muscle. However, in these patients with VVS, simply strengthening the muscle did not relieve their pain. On the other hand, the results of this important study indicated that stabilization of the pelvic floor muscle at rest was the key factor in alleviating vulvar pain.

Another recent report using the biofeedback technique looked at differentiating subtypes of vulvodynia patients from normals, based on readings of pelvic floor muscle stability. Importantly, the stability of the pelvic muscle at rest proved to be 92 percent accurate in identifying vulvodynia patients.[214] Other characteristics that reliably differentiated vulvodynia patients from normals included: the rate of onset of muscle contractions, the intensity of the muscle contractions, the speed at which the muscle returned to rest, the post-contraction resting baseline level, and the muscle fibers used during the contraction. For female patients with vulvodynia and VVS, we now are on the verge of a new technology that can be used to diagnose accurately their problem based upon physical findings or etiology rather than simply based upon a description of symptoms. Hopefully, the sEMG biofeedback technology will prove valuable in the accurate diagnosis of vulvodynia and VVS, and this will be the first of many new technologies applied to diagnosing and treating female sexual dysfunction.

The Vulvar Pain Foundation (VPF) serves women with chronic vulvar pain, providing information on research, treatment, emotional support, and opportunity to participate in research. Contact VPF at P.O. Drawer 177, Graham, NC 27253 (910-226-0704).

Vaginismus

Vaginismus consists of the recurrent, involuntary (uncontrollable) spasm of the outer third of the vagina. Since vaginismus interferes with intercourse, it is accompanied by embarrassment and frustration on the part of the female patient and significant stress for the couple. Vaginismus is less common than dyspareunia. Both of these dysfunctions account for less than 20 percent of the sexual complaints by females. Vaginismus probably accounts for 5 percent or less of female sexual complaints.[196] In making this diagnosis a careful history of the initial circumstances under which the symptoms appeared is very important. A careful physical exam is important as well. Once the vaginismus response is considered as the daignosis, treatment usually requires both a psychological and mechanical approach. Psychological factors include the following: past and present strong sexual inhibition; on rare occasion, sexual trauma, such as rape or incest; unexpressed negative feelings toward the sexual partner or the male figure; phobias about intercourse and/or sexual response.

The mechanical treatment usually involves educating the patient to the use of a series of graduated dilators combined with relaxation. A smaller dilator, approximately the size of the fifth finger, is first placed in the vagina by the woman. As each dilator is replaced by the next larger size without pain, change from muscle spasm to muscle relaxation occurs. Use of these dilators is not to cause actual mechanical dilation or stretching, but to enhance relaxation. Since the appropriate treatment frequently consists of a combination of the vaginal dilation exercises, one important step in the series of muscle awareness exercises is to help women develop an awareness of the sensation of the lower vagina, including the ability to recognize the distinction between a contracted and a relaxed pelvic floor muscle. Once the woman can identify clearly the appropriate muscles, isometric vaginal contractions can be done by the patient at home. Visual involvement of the partner is important, with the partner first using the dilators and then progressing ultimately to gradual insertion of the penis, with the woman's guidance increasingly controlling the pace and duration of the sexual activity.

For patients with severe phobias, additional techniques and a technique referred to as "systematic desensitization," under the guidance of a skilled therapist may be indicated. Some patients with milder forms have referred to self-help type text. An excellent book on the topic was written by Valins.[215]

Lifespan Experiences Affecting Women's Sexual Function

The most common lifespan experiences for women include menstruation and menopause. The majority of women, in addition, also become pregnant. The physiologic changes that accompany these areas and their impact on sexuality will be briefly discussed.

• **Menstrual Cycles.** It's been difficult to find any measureable correlation relating sexual desire and activity to the menstrual cycle phase. This has been particularly true when trying to correlate endocrine, hormonal levels, sexual activity, and sexual desire. For example, testosterone in women is the highest in the middle third of the cycle[216] while on the other hand sexual desire has been found in one study to be at its lowest point around mid-cycle, shortly after ovulation.[217] In that same study higher levels of sexual desire were reported in the phase leading up to ovulation. These findings point to the fact that women seem to demonstrate more variability and less predictability than men in the hormone-sexual behavior relationships. Correlations between average testosterone and sexual response in normal, healthy, premenopausal women have been difficult to find.[218] Researchers have to observe women with either low levels of testosterone, for example, those using certain oral contraceptives, or observe women with high levels of testosterone, to find the associations between sexual desire or behavior and testosterone levels.[219] In simpler terms, those women who have testosterone levels within a normal range do not as yet have a predictable level of sexual desire based solely on the absolute value of the testosterone level.

• **Pregnancy.** As pregnancy develops, sexual activity declines. There's very little data concerning sexual desire and responsiveness across the full term of pregnancy. One study found that the frequency of sexual relations decreased in the first trimester (mostly because of psychological factors, probably due to a misconception that intercourse during the first trimester might interrupt the pregnancy), increased in the second trimester (supposedly due to increased pelvic congestion), and decreased in the third trimester (because of physical discomfort).[19] On the other hand, most investigators have not been able to confirm an increase in sexual activity in the second trimester, although, the decrease in both the first and third trimesters has been confirmed. Currently, sexual intercourse and orgasm are thought to be safe for the fetus.

Postpartum, according to one prospective study of women who had just delivered their first child, sexual intercourse resumed in most of these women by the twelfth week after delivery.[220] Intercourse frequency was reduced probably in large part due to increased fatigue associated with care of the new baby.

Women who breast feed have not been studied extensively as far as evaluating the impact of lactation on a sexual response and sexual activity. One prospective study of women following the birth of their first child found that women who breast fed did not experience longterm sexual attitude or activity changes compared to levels before pregnancy. On the other hand, those same women, while they were breast feeding, were more likely to experience decreased sexual desire and enjoyment and an increase in pain with intercourse.[221] Interestingly, the authors of this study found an association between low androgen levels and loss of sexual desire. Since elevated prolactin (which occurs during the time of lactation and breast feeding) inhibits ovarian functioning, it is possible that the prolactin contributes to both low desire (testosterone decrease) and vaginal discomfort (estrogen decrease.) Not to be forgotten, however, are the psychosocial factors, including greater sleep deprivation and the need to remain more available to the infant. Occasionally the presence of depressive symptoms postpartum may play a role in the decreasing sexual desire. In addition, it's common for women to resume sexual activity postpartum "for their partner's sake" despite vaginal pain and discomfort. This naturally would contribute to decreased sexual interest.

• **Menopause And Hormone Replacement Therapy.** A decrease in sexual activity does occur in a significant number of post-menopausal women. A change in sexual activity cannot be ascribed to any specific hormonal changes of menopause.[222, 223] Studies that have compared and evaluated different gonadal (ovarian) steroids in menopausal women have led to the following observations. First, estrogen decreases are associated with decreased vaginal lubrication and atrophic vaginitis in about 10 percent of post-menopausal women. This lubrication problem may in turn cause pain with intercourse and decreased sexual interest. In addition, women who are more sexually active have less vaginal atrophy.[224] Providing the female with estrogen improves the vaginal lubrication and atrophic conditions, but it does not necessarily increase sex drive or activity. And finally, administering androgen (male hormones) has been shown to be associated with an increase in frequency of intercourse and an increase in orgasm only in surgically menopausal women.[225, 226]

At this point, one may be asking: "What contributes to sexual changes around menopause if hormonal factors do not play a major or consistent role?" The answer to this question and others similar will be made more clear and will result in improved clinical treatments in the near future as more research efforts and attention are turned to female sexual function and female sexual dysfunction. At the present time, aging seems to be a leading possibility. A decrease in the intensity of the female sexual response pattern accompanies aging. The patient then requires more direct and prolonged stimulation than during in earlier years. In most developed cultures in the world, aging brings a desexualization of women, which impacts the image the woman has of herself and that others have of her.[196] For those women in long-term relationships, the sexual patterns may have become uninteresting and routine. In addition, a middle-age woman's similarly middle-aged partner may have male sexual dysfunction problems that make sexual intercourse difficult and embarrasing. Often times, the years between 50 and 70 are marked with important and significant social changes, such as children leaving home and retirement. This necessitates the partners' re-examination of personal life values and interpersonal relationships. Sometimes the priority of sexuality in a person's life changes differently for the two partners when they recognize their loss of youth. In those cases the readjustment of the marital relationship is crucial, and recommitment is essential for enhancement and maintenance of the relationship.

Hormone replacement therapy, which involves estrogen or estrogen and progesterone compounds, without question appears to be helpful to sexual response by decreasing vaginal dryness and vaginal atrophy. This type of therapy also decreases other menopausal symptoms such as hot flashes, insomnia, headaches and certain memory losses. Reducing these symptoms helps women feel better. This feeling of well-being provides a healthier outlook and potentially allows the woman the chance to increase her interest in sex. The role of testosterone is still not fully clarified. For example, research suggests that fluctuations in the level of testosterone in young women has no particular effect on sexual desire. On the other hand, there's evidence that the loss of sexual desire caused by surgical removal of the ovaries (oophorectomy) in premenopausal women may be restored with the use of testosterone or a combination of testosterone and estrogen.[225, 226]

As stressed earlier, androgens, the male hormones such as testosterone, have been found to result in a more direct effect on sexual desire, sexual arousal, and the overall sense of well-being.[227] The most crucial issue is the long-term health effects on women who take androgens, particularly in terms of how they impact the cardiovascular system. Unfortunately, this is still a somewhat controversial area in that there's no clear evidence concerning this particular potential side effect. What is clearly needed is a better understanding of the basic science in this area so that non-hormonal drugs can be developed to improve sexual desire and arousal.

Pelvic Surgery

Without question, surgical procedures in the female genital area will have sexual implications. Postoperative discomfort and pain and some small amount of bloody secretions and discharge may be expected by the physician, but often causes alarm and considerable anxiety for the woman and her partner. It is very important for the physician to outline what sexual activities are permitted after the surgical procedure and which ones are prohibited and for how long. When a relatively longterm sexual or emotional adjustment is required following a major surgical procedure, it's always best to involve the partner in the preoperative discussions.

Hysterectomy

In theory, a small percentage of women may experience some physiologic differences in sex after removal of the uterus. For example, scar tissue may possibly prevent full ballooning of the vagina, which could make intercourse more difficult. Some women may possibly be troubled by the loss of uterine contractions and a diminished total vasocongestion at the time of arousal. When simultaneous removal of the ovaries (oophorectomy) is performed on a premenopausal woman, her available estrogen, as well as testosterone, are suddenly dramatically lowered with the possible impacts already mentioned from the role of these particular hormones. As we saw earlier, post-menopausal ovaries stop the production of estrogen, while they do however produce measureable quantities of testosterone and other androgens from the ovarian tissue. This testosterone and androgen production is obviously not available to women whose ovaries have been removed.

Certainly, the age of the women experiencing the surgery along with the reasons for a hysterectomy can be important variables contributing to sexual adjustment after surgery. For example, cancer surgery in younger women, who might otherwise have expected to have children, is likely to be more generally and sexually disruptive than surgery for benign disorders. Fortunately, most hysterectomies are performed for noncancerous, benign disorders (approximately 90 percent of the time).[228] When the hysterectomy procedure results in relief for the patient from symptoms such as chronic pain, excessive uterine bleeding or endometriosis, the patient usually has an improvement in quality of life measures and this impacts sexual function in a positive way.[226]

In general, the influence on sexual function of hysterectomy has been rather small. Some women may experience adverse psychological sequelae to hysterectomy, but most do not experience psychosexual problems postoperatively.[230] Those women who do develop problems are frequently those with simultaneous bilateral oophorectomy and resultant decreased estrogen secretion, as well as those who have preoperative sexual conflicts, or those who believe that a hysterectomy diminishes one's femininity. Women with post-op problems sometimes are poorly educated and have little understanding of the post-surgery hormonal change or what to expect afterwards. To minimize some of these postoperative problems, it's important for the patient to ask questions about effects of the surgery, as well as for the surgeon to assess the patient's psychological concerns and fears and potential effects on sexual response during the preoperative discussions. Some women who are at risk for adverse psychosexual problems certainly benefit from extra couseling before surgery.

Looking more specifically at a couple of studies that evaluated the effects of hysterectomy on sexual activity, one finds the results quite variable. For example, in one study, 97 women who had experienced hysterectomy were compared with 249 women of a similar age who had not had surgery.[229] Those women in the hysterectomy group reported more sexual satisfaction! Only 22 percent of the women who had hysterectomies, compared to 34 percent of the non-hysterectomy women, reported a sexual problem. For the women with hysterectomies, the variables that were found to be significant in explaining their sexual satisfaction in the order of relative importance during this study, were (1) the lack of other physiologic health problems, (2) the ability to reframe problems, and (3) the support of family and friends. In another study, women were observed before and after hysterectomies. All were undergoing hysterectomies for nonmalignant disorders and were monitored at three, six, and twelve months after surgery.[231] Of the 355 patients involved in this study, 49 percent reported "no interest in sexual activity" before surgery. At twelve months after surgery, 75 percent reported the same complaint. "No enjoyment of sexual activity" was reported by 44 percent of the women before surgery while 84 percent reported no enjoyment after surgery. Needless to say, this was a very large group of unhappy women in the post-surgery group. The results of this study also indicated that hysterectomy was in fact correlated with an increase in sexual complaints at six and twelve months after surgery and again revealed the variations between study groups. More studies are needed to clarify the reasons for increased sexual complaints post-hysterectomy.

Cancer

When a woman is diagnosed with cancer, initially the shock of the diagnosis has to be dealt with. Once treatment has begun, it is not unusual at all to experience anxiety about future sexual capacity. However, many women are reluctant to ask questions about sex. Therefore, the treating physician must communicate early on with the patient about the effects of the disease and its treatment on her sexuality.

Pelvic Cancer

Women diagnosed with gynecologic cancer are faced with both physiologic and psychologic effects of treatment. Psychological issues include fear of death, fear of partner's rejection, and fear of disfigurement. The physiologic side effects of treatment can be the result of surgery, radiation, or chemotherapy.

Cervical and endometrial cancer are treated by radical hysterectomy. As discussed earlier, this may possibly shorten the vagina and affect the woman's sexual response. Again, preoperative counseling about potential side effects of the surgery can help patients prepare for any postoperative changes and minimize the overall impact of those changes.

Colorectal cancer is the third leading cause of death from cancer in women in the United States.[232] When the rectum and distal colon are surgically removed, damage to the pelvic nerves may adversely affect sexual response. In addition, there may be a tendency for the posterior vaginal wall to lack the normal support after surgical removal of the rectum.

Cancer of the vulva may require extensive resection of the mons pubis, labia, or clitoris. This surgery may narrow the vaginal entrance, as well as alter physical appearance. Even the more conservative surgical resections with preservation of some normal anatomy may leave the patient with problems achieving orgasm. Similar cure rates for the conservative resection of the vulva versus the more radical vulvectomy have been encouraging and have led to reports that some women are capable of having orgasms after removal of the clitoris. On the other hand, there is still insufficient data to predict which women will be able to function and be capable of having orgasms following surgery for cancer of the vulva.

Pelvic exeneration may be required when cancer is either extensive or recurrent. This operation includes removal of the contents of the pelvis, to include removal of the rectum and lower bowel, as well as the bladder and vagina and uterus and ovaries. In addition to the negative factor of the cancer being extensive and requiring this radical procedure, the treatment will leave the patient with one or two stomas on her abdominal wall. These may occasionally smell of urine or flatus, thus contributing to a feeling of decreased sexuality and loss of self-esteem.

No sexual option after pelvic exeneration is perfect. In the absence of major vaginal reconstruction, the options include no sexual activity, direct penile-clitoral contact, use of a vibrator, masturbation, manual stimulation of the partner's genitals, and oral stimulation of the partner's genitals. No one decision is best for all couples. A given couple's age, previous sexual frequency, sexual attitudes, and each partner's level of enjoyment of past sexual activity will determine that couple's most acceptable options.

Chemotherapy may cause hair loss, disruption of bowel function, decrease in energy and atrophic changes of the vagina. All of these may affect sexual function by causing a decrease in sexual desire. Vaginal estrogen therapy, adequate medication for nausea and temporary utilization of wigs or head coverings may improve the patient's self-image and sexual function.

Radiation therapy is often used in treatment of cervical, endometrial, and vaginal cancer. It may produce significant changes to the vagina. The mucosa becomes atrophic, losing its elasticity, with decreases in length and width. In order to minimize some of these adverse effects, the patient may use vaginal dilators after the risk of hemorrhage has passed. Daily vaginal dilation by the patient will help prevent contracted scarring in the long term. Sexual activity should be encouraged once the patient has passed the point of risk for post-radiation bleeding.

Sometimes return to sexual activity is slowed by the sexual partner's fear that sex may actually injure the woman. Occasionally, the partner may fear actually contracting cancer or being affected by radiation. These are concerns to be dealt with by the treating physician before, during, and after the radiation therapy. Sexual rehabilitative couseling significantly increases the number of women who resume sexual activity after cancer treatment.

Breast Cancer

The sexual function problems associated with breast cancer in general, in mastectomy in particular, relate to the psychological and physiological effects of the disease and the treatment of the disease on the patient and the psychological effect on her partner. In many cases, the woman may feel deformed or mutilated, resulting in low self-esteem and inability to function sexually. In some cases the woman's loss of sexual function is related to her fear of rejection by her partner. Where sexual function is affected, therapeutic couseling may be of benefit. However, counseling the patient and her partner in advance about what to antici-pate after treatment for breast cancer no doubt provides the most service to the woman as a preventative measure. It is well-documented that a large proportion of emotional problems associated with mastectomy is due to the fact that the loss of the breast may have a negative impact on body image.[233] A number of studies have revealed that women who sought breast reconstruction were exhibiting evidence of positive coping and asserting effective problem solving behavior.[234, 235] Women who sought reconstruction after a mastectomy, in one study, were found to be more comfortable with their sexuality than before reconstruction.[236] Although the frequency of sexual activity did not increase, satisfaction did improve and more closely approached levels of satisfaction prior to mastectomy.

Oral chemotherapy with Nolvadex (tamoxifen citrate), a widely used chemotherapeutic agent for patients with breast cancer, has caused vaginal dryness in about a third of the patients. The FDA has recently approved this drug for reduction of the risk of breast cancer in women who are at high risk for the development of breast cancer based on their family history. This exciting new application could lead to millions of women preventing breast cancer through tamoxifen. Thus it is impera-tive that we develop an oral medication to treat vaginal dryness. On the other hand, tamoxifen evidently improves vaginal lubrication in some women, according to reports of women who were already suffering from vaginal dryness due to menopause. In these women, some reported that Nolvadex causes increased vaginal lubrication and possibly a clear discharge. This side effect of increased lubrication can be beneficial, obviously, to sexual activity.

The American Cancer Society's Reach to Recovery program offers support to breast cancer patients to help them adjust to their disease and treatment. The Young Women's Christian Association (YWCA) has developed a national program for post-op cancer patients, ENCORE (Encouragement, Normality, Counseling, Opportunity, Reaching Out, Energies Revived).

22
─────

SHE DOES WHAT?

Viagra and Apomorphine for Females

One of the most common questions we hear today is: Will Viagra work for females as well as for males? Based on our understanding of the mechanism of action of Viagra with its enhancement of the nitric oxide (NO) mechanism of smooth muscle relaxation that allows for increased blood flow, a couple of basic questions come to mind. First of all, is the same mechanism that we saw in the erectile tissue in the penis occurring in the erectile tissue of the clitoris and in the smooth muscle tissue of the vaginal wall? Since the arousal phase of female sexual function depends on increased blood flow into both the vaginal wall and the clitoris, any understanding of the basic physiology of those tissues may have predictive value on the role of Viagra. Recent reports from Goldstein, Krane, and colleagues[191, 192] have shown in the animal model in the laboratory that contraction of clitoral cavernosal and vaginal smooth muscle is regulated by adrenergic nerves. Relaxation of the clitoral cavernosal smooth muscle appears to be regulated mostly by the nitric oxide (NO) pathway. On the other hand, the mechanism of the vaginal smooth muscle relaxation appears to involve not only the NO pathway, but also other pathways. This opens up avenues for further research and further identification of mechanisms that might lead to drugs to affect additional pathways other than the nitric oxide pathway.

The same researchers in Boston have established in the laboratory a human clitoral smooth muscle cell culture model that allows character-ization of the function and biochemical pathways involved in the activity of those particular cells. Recently [192] human clitoral smooth muscle cells in culture were demonstrated to retain their structural and functional integrity as well as express the PDE type 5 functional receptors. Viagra blocks PDE 5. This information provides encouragement to the applica-tion of Viagra for improving the flow of blood during the arousal stage for the female.

Currently clinical studies are ongoing that will shed light on the safety as well as the efficacy of Viagra for females. As we saw earlier in the section on female sexual function that the arousal stage depends on increased blood flow to the vagina, as well as the clitoris. Viagra should be able to play an important role. You might suspect that females who because of vascular disease secondary to smoking, for example, have a compromised flow of blood to the pelvis and to the vaginal wall would not necessarily respond as well to Viagra as those females who have normal blood flow to the pelvis. Hopefully, by later in 1999 the answer to the question regarding the role of Viagra for the female will be answered.

Apomorphine

Apomorphine was discussed in Chapter 19 as a future option for oral treatment of male erectile dysfunction. This drug is also currently under investigation for use in treating female sexual dysfunction. It acts cen-trally, in the brain, and can be used in patients taking nitrates. Hopefully, there will be a role for these and other new oral medications in the near future for treatment of female sexual dysfunction.

23

PLANTS CAN STILL DO IT

Herbal Medicines for Females

There are a number of herbal remedies available for many different aspects of women's health. Problem areas for which there are herbal treatments range from vaginal dryness to hot flashes. In this chapter we will focus on those herbal treatments specifically utilized in the past that are geared toward improving sex drive, treating vaginal dryness, and treating noninfectious vaginitis. While this chapter is geared more toward specific areas of sexual dysfunction for which herbal remedies are available, it's important for the woman to have a good outlook on sexual activity. This is much easier if the woman is in excellent medical condition and includes a diet that will maximally provide nourishing foods, as well as minimize intake of ingredients such as caffeine and sugar. In addition, in order to optimize health, it's important to be physically active. It's also important to be able to relax and manage stress. There are numerous nutritional guides published elsewhere that outline courses of well balanced meals that provide adequate nutrition. Some of these courses do include herbal preparations that help provide that balanced diet.

I want to make it clear that I am not an expert on herbal remedies for men or women. However, in researching this book, it became obvious to me that many people rely on and have had some success with various herbs and plants for some of the symptoms and problems of sexual dysfunction. One of the best resources that I found on this subject is the book, *Natural Medicine for Menopause and Beyond* by Paula Maas, Susan Brown, and Nancy Bruning (Dell, 1997). Some of the summary material I have included in this chapter is explained in much greater detail in their excellent book.

Loss of Sexual Desire

As we have seen earlier, some psychological conditions such as depression and anxiety have a negative impact on sexual desire. These underlying problems need to be addressed first when there is a clearcut cause for decreased libido due to depression or anxiety. In addition, poor nutrition, fatigue, and stress can affect hormone levels and further reduce sexual desire. As we have seen earlier, hysterectomy and the hormonal changes associated with menopause, with the loss of production of estrogen and progesterone, as well as testosterone, contribute to a lack of sexual desire or arousal difficulties. In this group of women who are searching for more specific natural approaches, the following natural remedies may be helpful in addition to synthetic estrogens as hormone replacement therapy.[237]

• **Herbal Remedies.** Reputable herbalists avoid the traditional claims that astragalus, burdock, damiana, dong quai, false unicorn, ginseng, and kava are natural aphrodisiacs. However, several herbal preparations are available which contain a significant amount of plant hormone that may help improve libido. Herbal specialists recommend:

Black cohosh, licorice, and *red clover* are rich in plant estrogens. The usual dosage is one capsule or one-half to one teaspoon of a tincture up to three times a day.

Agnus castus, sarsaparilla root, wild yam root, and *yarrow flowers and leaves* are rich in plant progesterones. The usual dose is one capsule or one teaspoon of tincture up to three times a day.

• **Aromatherapy.** Several topical oils have been touted as aphrodisiacs in the past, but probably achieve their benefit by promoting relaxation and reducing anxiety.[237] There's no doubt a massage by a willing partner with body oils and baths containing one of the following aromatic oils may greatly reduce anxiety: *neroli, ylang-ylang, jasmine* and *rose oil.* Some women prefer rose oil which is considered more of a female aphrodisiac. This could explain a lot about the popularity of a bouquet of fresh roses in courtship!

• **Natural Hormone Therapy.** In some cultures around the world synthetic hormone replacement is utilized very little and large populations depend on the natural plant estrogen sources for hormone replacement. These sources for plant estrogen certainly are not harmful and are items that we have for years considered part of a well-balanced diet. In post-menopausal or post-hysterectomy women these should not be taken as an equal alternative to hormone replacement therapy with synthetic estrogens and progesterone. Much more research is needed to standardize dosages of plant hormones as compared to synthetic hormones and no doubt more data will be available in the future as to the specific benefits of a number of these sources of plant estrogens. Foods that are high in plant estrogens include:

Vegetables such as alfalfa (sprouts, powder, and plants), garlic, sprouting green peas, parsley, fennel, anise seeds, and celery.

Fruits, including dates, figs, apricots and apples.

Soybeans and soy based foods, including miso, tofu, and soy milk.

Legumes and nuts such as peanuts, almonds, and cashews. Flax seed is particularly high in lignins.

Whole grains such as oats, wheat, and corn.

Vaginal Dryness

As discussed earlier, women who are post-hysterectomy or who are in their post-menopausal years will have a tendency to have a thinning of the vaginal wall with increased dryness due to the decreased supply of estrogen. Not uncommonly, the blood supply to the entire genital area may decrease with atherosclerosis contributing to compromise in blood flow. These changes explain why intercourse can become uncomfortable and painful at times.

The conventional treatment for vaginal dryness is estrogen cream. This cream is applied to the vagina and the vulva. Usually, the patient notices a difference within one to two weeks. Some pupular nutritional supplements include Vitamin E, up to 600 IU daily for four to six weeks, to help treat atrophy of the vagina and increase lubrication. This is commonly taken orally, but may be applied directly to vaginal tissue. Essential fatty acids, such as gammalinoleic fatty acid (GLA), in doses up to 9 to 45 grams, three times a day. have been recommended by nutritionists. GLA, present in black currant oil, primrose oil, or borage oil supplements may also help with lubrication and possibly improve vaginal tissues. Essential fatty acids can be found in flax seeds and flax seed oil. A dose of one to three teaspoons per day may minimize symptoms within one month.

• **Herbal Remedies.** Additional herbal remedies may be helpful with vaginal thinning and dryness when they can help replace hormones. Herbal specialists [237] recommend for treatment of menopausal symptoms in general a preparation that contains *black cohosh, licorice,* and *mother wort.* This group seems to have a good track record for relieving vaginal dryness. The usual dose is one capsule or one teaspoon of tincture up to three times a day.

Vaginitis

Vaginitis is a condition where, due to an irritant, whether bacterial, yeast, noninfectious, such as related to douches or spermacides or sexual activity, the vaginal lining becomes irritated and there's a discharge of increased secretions from the vagina. A vaginal discharge is not necessarily a sign of illness, but one should make their physician aware and be treated appropriately. Based on what the irritative source may be, the consistency, color, and odor of the discharge will vary along with some other symptoms such as itching and burning. These changes are usually indicative of an overgrowth of a microorganism, whether bacterial or nonbacterial. When the irritative symptoms persist, even after treatment of an infection or in the absence of an infection, some women have found that certain herbal preparations have been effective.[237] The following herbal preparations, used either singly or in combination, have been popular for this problem:

Citrus seed extract, garlic, undecylenic acid and *aprylic acid* are popular oral herbal treatments.

Beth root, white poplar, cranesbill, and *false unicorn root* are useful for a discharge that is thin and watery. Take one teaspoon of tincture of these herbs up to three times daily for three months.[237]

Goldenseal and *cranesbill* may help reduce mucuslike discharge. Note, this is not to be taken instead of appropriate antibiotics per your physician. The usual dose of goldenseal and cranesbill is one-half to one teaspoon of tincture up to three times a day. It's been recommended to continue these herbs for a month after symptoms have cleared.

Goldenseal and *echinacea* together or *blue cohosh, comfrey, raspberry leaf,* or *oatstraw* have been utilized for vaginitis, as well. When the problem is chronic, *St. John's wort,* one cup for irrigation, or as an extract (1 teaspoon) up to three times, a day has been recommended.[237]

For the application of herbal preparations for vaginal douche, a general formula for vaginitis is two teaspoons each of powdered *goldenseal* and *myrrh* plus one-half teaspoon of *ginger* per pint of water. This preparation has been recommended with first boiling the herbs, letting the solution cool, followed by straining the formula. At that point the strained formula is recommended once a day until symptoms clear. Some herbalists add *calendula* for tissues that are extremely irritated.

At this point I need to say I have no experience in recommending any of these personally to any of my patients, but there are excellent references available that summarize these and other herbal remedies for female sexual dysfunction problems discussed in this chapter.[237] Hopefully, in the future more scientific studies will be done that will isolate the active ingredients from some of these preparations and use those isolates in scientifically designed clinical trials and give us better answers to how to apply these materials for the best treatment of our patients.

24

WHAT'S LOVE GOT TO DO WITH IT?

Healthy Relationships
and Sexual Function

Wat is love? Descriptions are found in ancient sacred texts, classic literature, and mythology as well as in today's popular songs, movies, and books in every language. If you have read this far, you know this book is about physical and psychological causes and treatments of male and female sexual dysfunction. However, you have also observed that many of the treatments discussed so far are more effective—often *only* effective—if applied in the context of a caring, loving sexual relationship.

I am a medical doctor, specifically a urologist, not a sex therapist or a pyschologist. However, I have witnessed time and time again in my own practice the importance of good relationships in maintaining normal sexual function for both the male and female. We have seen in the discussions of sexual dysfunction for both male and female that the quality of the relationship with their partner is the key to normal sexual function.

Every day we see couples who have been married for 40 years who were high school sweethearts who fell in love as teenagers and have maintained an excellent relationship for a long period of time. When couples such as this come into our office with a sexual dysfunction problem for either the male or female, the solution to that problem is made much more easy by the fact that they have excellent support from their partner.

On the other hand, whenever there is a problem with the relationship, regardless of its cause or source, it invariably affects sexual function. In those cases, the relationship problems have to be solved first. In the seventies, a best-selling book on relationships and self-esteem popularized the phrase, "I'm okay, you're okay." Recently, a patient gave this expression an interesting twist with respect to healthy sexual functioning within a loving relationship: "When we're okay, I'm okay." There is a lot of wisdom in those few words.

Can you have sex without love? Certainly. One study of teenage boys showed that up to 70 percent thought it was okay to tell a girl that they loved her just so they could have sex with her. That survey obviously was done with a rather immature age group. But were those teenage boys simply immature, or were they driven totally by their testosterone level?

As urologists, we can fix the hydraulics for the male to treat his erectile dysfunction; however, his overall sexual function totally depends upon the quality of his relationship with his partner. Little everyday things perk up the relationship: those thoughtful things such as taking out the garbage or helping out around the house without being asked, spending less time on the sofa watching TV, and not dedicating every weekend to sports. These are steps in the right direction to strengthen a relationship, and will be considered romantic by many females. The best part about these simple, little things one can do to improve the relationship is that they don't cost much money.

Yes, flowers and clothes and perfume are great, but quality time is the key. Couples who make an effort to improve communication and therefore improve their relationship on a daily basis lay the foundation for strengthening the relationship and maintaining normal sexual function.

So, what does love have to do with it? Everything!

Notes

1. Brenot PH: Male Impotence - A historical Perspective. L'Esprit du Temps, France, 1994.
2. Deysach LJ: Comparative morphology of erectile tissue of penis with especial emphasis on probable mechanism of erection. Am J Anat 1939; 64:111.
3. Christensen GC: Angioarchitecture of the canine penis and the process of erection. Am J Anat 1954; 95:227-250.
4. Newman HF Northrup JD, Devlin I: Mechanism of human penile erection. Invest Urol 1964; 1:350-353.
5. Dorr L, Brody M: Hemodynamic mechanisms of erection in the canine penis. Am J Physiol 1967; 213:1526.
6. Shirai M, Ishii N, Mitsukawa S, et al.: Hemodynamic mechanism of erection in the humas penis. Arch Androl 1978; 1:345-349.
7. Wagner G: Erection, physiology and endocrinology. In Wagner G, Green R, eds: Impotence: Physiological and Surgical Diagnosis and Treatment. New York, Plenum Press, 1981, 25 - 36.
8. Lue T: Physiology of Penile Erection and Pathophysiology of Erectile Dysfunction and Priapism. Campbell's Urology 1998; 7:1157-1174
9. Hsu GL, Brock G, Martinez-Pipeiro L, et al.: The three-dimensional structure of the human tunica albuginea: Anatomical and ultrastructural levels. Int J Impotence Res 1992; 4:117-129.
10. Levine LA. erectile dysfunction: Causes, diagnosis and treatment. Compr Ther. 1989; 15: 54-58.
11. Marson L. Platt KB, McKenna KE: Central nervous system innervation of the penis as revealed by the transneuronal transport of pseudorabies virus. Neuroscience 1993; 55:280.
12. Althof SE, Seftel AD: The evaluation and management of erectile dysfunction. Psychiatr. Clin N Am 1995; 18:171-172

13. Greiner KA, Weigel JW: Erectile dysfunciton. Am Fam Physician. 1996; 54:1675-1682.
14. Boolell M, Gepi-Atlee S, Gingell JC, Allen MJ: sildenafil, a novel effective oral therapy for male erectile dysfunciton. Br. J. Urol. 1996; 78:257-261
15. Lue TF, Takamura T, Schmidt RA, et al.: Hemodynamics of erection in the monkey. J Urol 1983; 130:1237-1241.
16. NIH Consensus Development Panel on Impotence. Impotence: NIH Consensus conference. JAMA. 1993; 270:83-90
17. Feldman HA, Goldstein I, Hatzichristou DG, Krane RJ, McKinley JB: Impotence and its medical and psychosocial correlates: results of the Massechusetts Male Aging Study. J Urol 1994; 151:54-61.
18. United States Bureau of the Census, 1992.
19. Masters WH, Johnson V: Human Sexual Response. Boston, Little, Brown, 1970.
20. Dewire DM: Evaluation and treatment of erectile dysfunction. Am Fam Physician 1996; 53:2101-2107.
21. Goldstein I, Feldman MI, Deckers PJ, et al: Radiation - associated impotence: a clinical study of its mechanism. JAMA 1984; 251:903-910.
22. Rosen MP, Greenfield AJ, Walker TG, et al: Arteriogenic impotence: findings in 195 impotent men examined with selective internal pudendal angiography. Radiology 1990; 174:1043-1048.
23. Levine FJ, Greenfield AJ, and Goldstein I: Arteriographically determined occlusive diseae within the hypogastric-cavernous bed in impotent patients following blunt perineal and pelvic trauma J Urol 1990; 144:1147-1153.
24. Rosen MP, Greenfield AJ, Walker TG, et al: Cigarette smoking: An independent risk factor for athersclerosis in the hypogastric-cavenous arterial bed of men with arteriogenic impotence. J Urol 1991; 145:759-763.

25. Hseih JT, Muller SC, and Lue. TF: The influence of blood flow and blood pressure on penile erection. Int J Impotence Res 1989; 1: 35-42.

26. Rajfer J, Rosciszewski A, and Mehringer M: Prevalence of corporal venous leakage in impotent men. J of Urol 1988; 140: 69-71.

27. Christ GJ, Maayani S, Valcic M, Melman A: Pharmacologic studies of human erectile tissue: Characteristics of spontaneous contractions and alterations in alpha-adrenoceptor responsiveness with age and disease in isolated tissues. Br J Pharmocol 1990; 101: 375-381.

28. Juenemann KP, Lue TF, Luo JA, et al: The effect of cigarette smoking on penile erection. J Urol 1987; 138: 438-441.

29. Bancroft J, and Wu FC: Changes in erectile responsiveness during androgen replacement therapy. Arch Sex Behav 1983; 12: 59-66.

30. Graham CW, and Regan JB: Blinded clinical trial of testosterone enanthate in impotent men with low or low-normal serum testosterone levels. Int J Impotence Res 1992; 4:144.

31. Leonard MP, Nickel CJ, and Morales A: Hyperprolactinemia and impotence: why, when and how to investigate. J Urol 1989; 142: 992-994.

32. Finkle AL, Taylor SP: Sexual potency after radical prostatectomy. J Urol 1981; 125:350.

33. Walsh PC, Lepor H, Eggleston JC: Radical prostatectomy with preservation of sexual function: Anatomical and pathological considerations. Prostate 1983; 4:473.

34. Fowler JE Jr, Clayton M, Sharifi R, et al: Early experience with Walsh technique of radical retropubic prostatectomy. Urology 1987; 29: 242.

35. Lue TF: Impotence after radical pelvic surgery: Physiology and management. {Review} Urol Int 1991; 46:259.

36. Quinlen DM, Epstein JI, Carter BS, et al: Sexual function following radical prostatectomy: influence of preservation of neu-rovascular bundles. J Urol 1991; 145: 998.

37. Catalona WJ: Patient selection for, results of, and impact on tumor resection of potency-sparing radical prostatectomy. Urol Clin North Am 1990; 17: 819.

38. Madorsky ML, Ashamalla MG, Schussler I, et al: Post prostatectomy impotence. J Urol 1976; 115: 401.

39. Lindner A. Golomb J, Korzcak D, et al: Effects of prostatectomy on sexual function. Urology 1991; 37: 26.

40. Nevelsteen A, Beyens G, Duchateau J, et al: Aortofemoral reconstruction and sexual function: A prospective study. Eur J Vasc Surg 1990; 4: 247.

41. Bauer JJ, Gelernt IM, Salky B, et al: Sexual dysfunction following proctocolectomy for benign disease of the colon and rectum. Ann Surg, 1983; 197:363.

42. Cunsolo A, Bragaglia RB, Manara G, et al: Urogenital dysfunction after abdominoperineal resection for carcinoma of the rectum. Dis Colon Rectum, 1990; 33:918.

43. Wein AJ, Van Arsdalen K: Drug-induced male sexual dysfunction. Urol Clin North Am 1988: 15:23-31.

44. Benet AE, and Melman A: The epidemiology of erectile dysfunction. Urol Clin North Am, 1995; 22: 699-709.

45. Zinreich ES, Devogatis LR, Herpst J, et al: Pre and post treatment evaluation of sexual function in patients with adenocarcinoma of the prostate. Int J Radiat Oncol Bio Phys, 1990; 19:729.

46. Goldstein I, Feldman MI, Deckers PJ, et al: Radiation-associated impotence. A clinical study of its mechanism. JAMA, 1984; 251:903.

47. Nowlin NS, Brick JE, Weaver DJ, et al: Impotence in scleroderma. Ann Intern Med 1986; 104:794.

48. Abrams HS, Hester LR, Sheridan WF, et al: Sexual functioning in patients with chroniic renal failure. J Nerv Ment Dis, 175; 160:220.

49. Cornely CM, Schade RR, Van Thiel DH, et al: Chronic advanced liver disease and impotence: cause and effect? Hepatology,

1984;4:1227.

50. Faugier J, Wright S: Homophobia, stigma and AIDS - an issue for all health care workers. Nursing Practice, 1990; 3:27.

51. Welby SB, Rogerson SJ, Beeching NJ: Autonomic neuropathy is common in human immunodefieciency virus infection. J Infect, 1991; 23:123.

52. Zeiss AM, Davies HD, Wood M, et al: The incidence and correlates of erectile problems in patients with Alzheimer's disease. Arch Sex, Behav, 1990; 19:325.

53. Fletcher EC, Martin RJ: Sexual dysfunction and erectile impotence in chroinic obstructive pulmonary disease. Chest, 1982; 81:413.

54. Patchell RA, Fellows HA, Humphries LL: Neurologic complications of anorexia nervosa. Acta Neurol Scand, 1994; 80:111.

55. Ono N, Lumpkin MD, Samson WK, et al: Intrahypothalamic action of corticotropin-releasing factor (CRF) to inhibit growth hormone and LH release in the rat. Life Science, 1984; 35:1117.

56. O'Leary MP, Fowler FJ, Lenderking WR, et al: Brief male sexual function inventory for Urology. Urology, 1995; 46:697.

57. Davis-Joseph B, Tiefer L, Melman A: Accuracy of the initial history and physical examination to establish the etiology of erectile dysfunction. Urology, 1995; 45:498.

58. Lue TF: Impotence: A patient's goal-directed approach to treatment. Work J. Urol, 1990; 8:67.

59. Brock G, Lue TF: Impotence: A patient's goal-directed approach. Monogr Urol, 1992; 13:99.

60. Lue TF: Editorial comment. J Urol 1994a; 152:1661.

61. Dormont P: Life Events That Predispose to Erectile Dysfunction. Medical Aspects of Human Sexuality, 1989; 23:17.

62. Fischer C: Cycle of penile erection synchronous with dreaming sleep. Arch Gen Psychiatry, 1965; 12:29.

63. Karacan I: Clinical value of nocturnal penile erection in the prognosis of impotence. Med Aspects Hum Sexuality, 1970;

4:27.

64. Barry JM, Blank B, Boileau M: Nocturnal penile tumescence monitoring with stamps. Urology, 1980; 15:171.

65. EK A, Bradley WE, Krane RJ: Nocturnal penile rigidity measured by the snap-gauge band. J Urol, 1983; 129:964.

66. Allen R, Brendler CB: Snap-gauge compared to a full nocturnal penile tumescence study for evaluation of patients with erectile impotence. J Urol, 1990; 143:51.

67. Carroll JL, Baltish MH, Bagley DH: The use of Potentest in the multidisciplinary evaluation of impotence: Is it a reliable measure? Jefferson Sexual Function Center. Urology, 1992; 39:226.

68. Diedrich GK, Stock W, Lo Piccolo J: A study on the mechanical reliability of the Dacomed snap gauge: Implications for the differentiation between organic and psychogenic impotence. Arch Sex Behav, 1992; 21:509.

69. Colombo F, Fenice O, Austoni E: NPT: Nocturnal penile tumescence test. Arch Ital Urol Androl, 1994; 66:159.

70. Bradley WE, Trimm GW, Gallagher JM, Johnson BK: New method for continuous measurement of nocturnal penile tumescence and rigidity. Urology, 1985; 26:4.

71. Hirshkowitz M, Ware JC: Studies of nocturnal penile tumescence and rigidity. In Singer C, Weiner WJ, eds: Sexual Dysfunction: A Neuro-Medical Approach. Armonk, NY, Futura Publishing Company, Inc., 1994;77-99.

72. Ellenberg M: Impotence in diabetes: the neurologic factor. Ann Intern Med, 1971; 75:213.

73. McCulloch DK, Campbell IW Wu FC, et al: The prevalence of diabetic impotence. Diabetologia, 1980; 18:279.

74. Spark RF, White RA, Connolly PB: Impotence is not always psychogenic: Newer insights into hypothalamic-pituitary-gonadal dysfunction. JAMA; 1980; 243:750.

75. Lustman PJ Clouse RE: Relationship of psychiatric illness to impotence in men with diabetes. Diabetes Care, 1990;13:893.

76. Diabetes Control and Complications Trial

Research Group: The effect of intensive treatment of diabetes on the development and progression of long-term conplications in insulin-dependent diabetes mellitus. N Engl J Med, 1993; 329:977.

77. Molitch ME, Elton RL, Blackwell RE, et al: Bromocriptine as primary therapy for prolactin-secreting macroadenomas: results of a prospective multicenter study. J Clin Endocrinol Metab, 1985; 60:698.

78. McClure RD, Oses R, Ernest ML: Hypogonadal impotence treated by transdermal testosterone. Urology, 1991; 37:224.

79. McClure RD, Marshall G; Endocrinologic sexual dysfunction. In Singer C, Weiner WJ (eds): Sexual Dysfunction: A Neuro-Medical Approach. Armonk, NY, Futura Publishing Company, 1994, 245-273.

80. Sato Y, Horita H, Kurohata T, Adachi H, and Tsukamoto T: Effect of Testosterone Replacement on Extracellular Nitric Oxide in the PVN in aged rats.. J Urol, 1998; 159, No. 5, Supplement, Abstr # 381.

81. Morales A, Johnston B, Heaton JW, et al: Oral androgens in the treatment of hypogonadal impotent men. J Urol, 1994; 152:1115.

82. Virag R: Intracavernous injection of papaverine for erectile failure. Lancet, 1982; 2:938.

83. Juneman KP, Alken P: Pharmacotherapy of erectile dysfunction: a review. Int J Impot Res, 1989; 1:71.

84. Stief CG, Wetterauer U: Erectile responses to intracavernous papaverine and phentolamine: comparison of single and combined delivery. J Urol, 1988; 140:1415.

85. Cooper AJ: Evaluation of I-C papaverine in patients with psychogenic and organic impotence. Can J Psychiatry, 1991; 36:574.

86. Zorgniotti AW, Lefleur RS: Auto-injection of the corpus cavernosum with a vasoactive drug combination for vasculogenic impotence. J Urol, 1985; 133:39.

87. Goldstein I, Payton T, Padma-Nathan H: Therapeutic roles of intracavernous papaverine. Cardiovasc Intervent Radiol, 1988; 11:237.

88. Kerfoot WW, Carson CC: Pharmacologically induced erections among geriatric men. J Urol, 1991; 146:1022.

89. Roy AC, Adaikan PG, Sen DK, Ratnam SS: Prostaglandin 15-hydroxydehydrogenase activity in human penile corpora cavernosa and its significance in prostaglandin-mediated penile erection. Br J Urol, 1989; 64:180.

90. van Ahlen H, Peskar BA, Sticht G, Hertfelder HJ: Pharmacokinetics of vasoactive substances administered into the human corpus cavernosum. J Urol, 1994; 151:1227.

91. Stackl W, Hasun R, Marberger M: Intracavernous injection of prostaglandin E_1 in impotent men. J Urol, 1988; 140:66.

92. Lea AP, Bryson HM, Balfour JA: Intracavernous alprostadil. A review of its pharmacodynamic and pharmacokinetic properties and therapeutic potential in erectile dysfunction. Drugs Aging, 1996; 8:56.

93. Linet OI, Ogrine FG, for the Alprostadil Study Group. Efficacy and Safety of intracavernosal alprostadil in men with erectile dysfunction. N Engl J Med, 1996; 334:873.

94. Bennett AH, Carpenter AJ Barada JH: An improved vasoactive drug combination for a pharmacological erection program. J Urol, 1991; 146:1564.

95. Padma-Nathan H, Hellstrom WJG, Kaiser FE, et al: Treatment of men with erectile dysfunction with transurethral alprostadil. N Engl J Med, 1997; 336:1.

96. Sidi AA, Lewis JH: Clinical trial of a simplified vacuum erection device for impotence treatment. Urology, 1992; 39:526.

97. Lewis RW, Witherington R. External vacuum therapy for erectile dysfunction: use and results. World J Urol. 1997; 15:78.

98. Marmar JL, DeBenedictis TJ, Praiss DE: The use of a vacuum constriction device to augment a partial erection following an intracavernous injection. J Urol, 1988; 140:975.

99. Korenman SG, Viosca SP: Use of a vacuum tumescence device in the management of

impotence in men with a history of penile implant or severe pelvic disease. J Am Geriatr Soc, 1992; 40:61.

100. Sidi AA, Becker EF, Zhang G, et al: Patient acceptance of and satisfaction with an external negative pressure device for imptence. J Urol, 1990; 144:1154.

101. Metz P: Arteriogenic erectile impotence. Dan Med Bull, 1986; 33:134.

102. Lewis RW: Vascular surgery in the management of erectile dysfunction. In Rous SN, ed: A Urology Annual. East Norwalk, CT, Appleton and Lang, 1990, 1-25.

103. Lewis RW: Venous ligation surgery for venous leakage. Int J Impotence Res, 1990; 2:1.

104. Lewis RW: Venous surgery in the patient with erectile dysfunction. Urol Clin North Am, 1993; 1:21-38.

105. Sohn MH, Sikora RR, Bohndorf KK, et al: Objective follow-up after penile revascularization. Int J Impotence Res, 1992; 4:73.

106. Hatzichristou D, Goldstein I: Penile microvascular and arterial bypass surgery. Urol Clin North Am, 1993; 1:39-60.

107. Goldstein I, Hatzichristow DG, Pescatori EG: Pelvic, perineal, and penile trauma-associated arteriogenic impotence: pathophysiologic mechanisms and the role of microvascular arterial bypass surgery. In Bennet AH, ed: Impotence - Diagnosis and Management of Erectile Dysfunction. Philadelphia, W.B. Saunders Company, 1994; 213-228.

108. Sharlip ID: Vasculogenic impotence secondary to atherosclerosis/dysplasia. In Bennett AH, ed: Impotence - Diagnosis and Management of Erectile Dysfunction. Philadelphia, WB Saunders Company, 1994, 205-212.

109. Donatucci CF, Lue TF: Venous Surgery: Are we kidding ourselves? In Lue TF, ed: World Book of Impotence. London, Smith-Gordon and Company, 1992, 221-227.

110. Lewis RW; Arteriovenous surgeries: Do they make any sense? In Lue TF, ed: World Book of Impotence. Lordon, Smith-Gor-don and Company, 1992, 199-220.

111. Lewis RW: Venogenic impotence: Is there a future? Curr Opin Urol, 1994; 6:340.

112. Wespes E, Schulman C: Venous impotence: Pathophysiology, diagnosis and treatment. J Urol, 1993; 149:1238.

113. Motiwala HG, Patel DD, Joshi SP, Baxi HM, Desai KD, Shah KN. Experience with penile venous surgery. Urol Int., 1993; 51:9.

114. Stief CG, Djamilian M, Truss MC, Tan H, Thon WF, Jonas U: Prognostic factors for the postoperative outcome of penile venous surgery for venogenic erectile dysfunction. J Urol, 1994; 151:880.

115. Bogoras NA: Uber d:e volle plastiche Wiederherstellung eines rum Koitus fahigen Penis (Peniplastica totalis). Zentralbl/Chir 1936; 63:1271.

116. Bergman RT, Howard AH, Barnes RW: Plastic reconstruction of the penis. J Urol, 1948; 59:1174.

117. Bett WR: The os penis in man and beast. Proc Roy Soc Med, 1951; 44:433.

118. Frumpkin AP: Reconstruction of the male genitalia. Am Rev Soviet Med, 1944; 2:14.

119. Goodwin WE, Scott WW: Phalloplasty. J Urol, 1952; 68:903.

120. Loeffler RA, Sayegh ES: Perforated acrylic implants in the management of organic impotence. J Urol, 1960; 84:559.

121. Loeffler RA, Savegh ES, Lash H: The artificial os penis. Plastic Reconst Surg, 1964; 34:71.

122. Beheri GE: Beheri's operation for treatment of impotence — observations on 125 cases. Kasr el Aini J Surg, 1960; 1:390.

123. Beheri GE: The problem of impotence solved by a new surgical operation. Kasr el Aini J Surg, 1960; 1:50.

124. Beheri GE: Surgical treatment of impotence. Plast Reconst Surg, 1966; 38:92.

125. Grabstald H: Postradical cystectomy impotence treated by penile silicone implant. NY State J Med, 1970; 70:23.

126. Lash H: Silicone implant for impotence. J Urol, 1968; 100:709.

127. Pearman RO: Treatment of organic impotence by implantation of a penile prosthesis. J Urol, 1967; 97:716.

128. Small MP, Carrion HM, Gordon JA: Small-Carrion penile prosthesis: new implant for management of impotency. Urology, 1975; 5:479.

129. Finney RP: New hinged silicone penile implant. J Urol, 1977; 118:585.

130. Jonas U, Jacobi GH: Silver-silicone penile prosthesis. J Urol, 1980; 123:865.

131. Kaufman JJ: Penile prosthetic surgery under local anesthesia. J Urol, 1982; 123:1190.

132. Scott FB, Bradley WE, Trimm GW: Management of erectile impotence: use of implantable inflatable prosthesis. Urology, 1973; 2:80.

133. Montague DK, Barada JH, Belker AM, et al. Clinical Guidelines Panel on Erectile Dysfunction: summary report on the treatment of organic erectile dysfunction. J Urol. 1996; 156:2007.

134. Fishman IJ, Culha M, and Scott FB: Sixteen Year Experience in the Management of Infected Penile Prosthesis Utilizing the Rescue Procedure. J Urol, 1998; 159, No. 5, Supplement, Abst # 1053.

135. Gelbard MK, Dorey F, James K: The natural history of Peyronie's disease. J Urol, 1990; 144:1376.

136. Kim JH, Carson CC: Development of Peyronie's disease with the use of vacuum constriction device. J Urol, 1993; 149:1314.

137. Gelbard MK, James K, Reich P, Dorey F: Collagenase versus placebo in the treatment of Peyronie's disease: A double-blind study. J Urol, 1993; 146:56.

138. Levine LA, Merrick PF, Lee RC: Intralesional verapamil injection for the treatment of Peyronie's disease. J Urol 1994; 151:1522.

139. Carson CC, Coughlin PWF: Radiation therapy for Peyronie's disease: Is there a place? J Urol 1985; 134:684.

140. Coughlin PWF, Carson CC, Parrlson DF: Surgical correction of Peyronie's disease: The Nesbitt procedure. J Urol 1984; 131: 282.

141. Horton CE, Devine CJ Jr: Peyronie's disease. Plast Reconstr Surg, 1973; 52:503.

142. Lue TF: Penile Venous Surgery. Urol Clin North Am 1989; 16:607.

143. Moatague DK, Lakin MM: Erectile prosthesis in Peyronie's disease. Presented at the International Conference on Peyronie's Disease. Bethesda, 1993.

144. Hengeveld MW: Erectile disorder: A psychosexological review. In Jones U, Thon WF, Stief CG, eds: Erectile Dysfunction. Berlin, Springer-Verlag, 1991, 207-220.

145. McCulloch DK, Hosking DJ, Tobert A: A pragmatic approach to sexual dysfunction in diabetic men: psychosexual counseling. Diabet Med. 1986, 3:485.

146. Kaplan HS: The New Sex Therapy. New York, Brunner/Mazel, 1974.

147. Kaplan HS: The Evaluation of Sexual Disorders. New York, Brunner/Mazel, 1983.

148. Sussett JG, et al. "Effect of Yohimbine Hydrochloride on Erectile Impotence: A Double-Blind Study," J Urol 1989; 141:1360-3.

149. Morales A, et al. "Is Yohimbine Effective in the Treatment of Organic Impotence? Results of a Controlled Trial. J Urol 1987; 137:1168-72

150. Betz J, White KD, and der Marderosian AH. "Chemical Analysis of 26 Commercial Yohimbe Products." J Am Chem Soc 1995; 89:1189-94.

151. Duke JA: Handbook of Medicinal Herbs (Boca Raton: CBC Press, 1985).

152. Waynberg J: "Aphrodisiacs: Contribution to the Clinical Validation of the Traditional Use of Ptychopetalum Guyanna," Presented at The First International Congress on Ethnopharmacology, Strasbourg, France, June 5-9, 1990.

153. Sikora R, et al: "Ginkgo Biloba Extract in the Therapy of Erectile Dysfunction," J Urol 1989; 141:188A.

154. Sohn M and Sikora R: "Ginkgo Biloba Extract in the Therapy of Erectile Dysfunction," J Sex Educ Ther 1991; 17:53-61.

155. Shibata S, Tanaka O, Shoji J, and Saito H: "Chemistry and Pharmacology of Panax," Economic and Medicinal Plant Research 1985; 1:217-84.

156. Kim C, Choi H, Kim CC, et al: "Influence of Ginseng on Mating Behavior of Male Rats," Am J Chinese Med 1976; 4:163-8.

157. Fahim WS, Harman JM, Clevenger TE, et al: "Effect of Panax Ginseng on Testosterone Level and Prostate in Male Rats," Arch Androl 1982; 8:261-3.

158. White JR, et al: "Enhanced Sexual Behavior in Exercising Men," Arch Sex Behav 1990; 19:193-209.

159. Boolell M, Allen MJ, Ballard SA, et al: Sildenafil: an orally active type 5 cyclic GMP-specific phosphodiesterase inhibitor for the treatment of penile erectile dysfunction. Int J Impot Res. 1996; 8:47-52.

160. Jeremy JY, Ballard SA, Naylor AM, Miller MA, Angelini GD. Effects of sildenafil, a type-5 cGMP phosphodiesterase inhibitor, and Papaverine on cyclic GMP and cyclic AMP levels in the rabbit corpus cavernosum in vitro. 1997 Br J Urol; 79: 958-963.

161. O'Leary MP: Cautions in the use of oral agents for the management of erectile dysfunction 1998 AUA News; Vol 3, No. 4, p 20.

162. Eardley I, Morgan RJ, Dinsmore WW, Pearson J, Wulff MB, Boolell M. UK-92,480, a new oral therapy for erectile dysfunction, a double-blind, placebo-controlled trial with treatment taken as required. In: Proceedings of the 91st annual meeting of the American Urological Association; May 4-9, 1996; Orlando, Fla. Abst 737.

163. Gingell CJC, Jardin A, Olsson AM, et al. UK-92,480, a new oral treatment for erectile dysfunction: a double-blind, placebo-controlled, once daily dose response study. In: Proceedings of the 91st annual meeting of the American Urological Association; May 4-9, 1996; Orlando, Fla. Abst 738.

164. Goldstein, et al: Oral Sildenafil in the Treatment of Erectile Dysfunction, New Engl J Med, 1998; 338:1397.

165. Padma-Nathan H, and the Sildenafil Study Group: A 24-week, fixed-dose study to assess the efficacy and safety of Sildenafil (Viagra) in men with erectile dysfunction. J Urol, 1998; 159, No. 5, Supplement, Abst # 911.

166. Steers WD, and the Sildenafil Study Group: Meta-analysis of the efficacy of Sildenafil (Viagra) in the treatment of severe erectile dysfunction. J Urol 1998; 159, No. 5, Supplement, Abst # 910.

167. Wagner G, Analysis of the efficacy of Sildenafil (Viagra) in the treatment of male erectile dysfunction in elderly patients. J Urol 1998; 159, No. 5, Supplement, Abst # 912.

168. Gwinup G. Oral phentolamine in nonspecific erectile insufficiency. Ann Intern Med. 1988; 109:162-163.

169. Zorgniotti AW. Experience with buccal phentolamine mesylate for impotence. Int J Impot Res. 1994; 6:37-41.

170. Goldstein I and the Vasomax Study Group: Efficacy and safety of oral phentolamine (Vasomax) for the treatment of minimal erectile dysfunction. J Urol 1998; 159, No. 5, Supplement, Abst #919.

171. Lipschultz LI: Injection therapy for erectile dysfunction N Engl J Med. 1996; 334:913-914.

172. Heaton JPW, Morales A, Adams MA, Johnston B, El-Rashidy R. Recovery of erectile function by the oral administration of apomorphine. Urology. 1995; 45: 200-206.

173. Lal S, Laryea E, Thavundayil JX, et al. Apomorphine-induced penile tumescence in impotent patients: preliminary findings. Prog Neuropsychopharmacol Biol Psychiatry. 1987; 11:235-242.

174. Lal S, Tesfaye Y, Thavundayil JX, et al. Apomorphine: clinical studies on erectile impotence and yawning. Prog Neuropsychopharmocol Biol Psychiatry. 1989; 13:329-339.

175. Padma-Nathan H, Fromm-Freeck S, Ruff DD, McMurray JG, Rosen RC, and the Apmorphine SL Study Group: Effi-

cacy and safety of apomorphine SL vs placebo for male erectile dysfunction (med). J Urol 1998; 159, No. 5, Supplement, Abst # 920.

176. Chuang AT, Strauss JD, Murphy RA and Steers, WD: Sildenafil specifically amplifies endogenous cGMP-dependent relaxation and uncouples force form myosin light chain phosphorylation in rabbit corpus cavernosum smooth muscle. J Urol 1988; 159, No. 5, Supplement, Abst #365.

177. Lue TF, Rashwan HM, and El-Sakka AI: Outcome analysis of correcting penile deformity with incision and venous grafting. J Urol 1998; 159, No. 5, Supplement, Abst #453.

178. Reidl CR, Plas E, Engelhardt P, and Pfulger H: Iontophoresis for the treatment of Peyronie's disease. J Urol 1998; 159, No. 5, Supplement, Abst #451.

179. Schiavi RC and Segraves RT: The Biology of Sexual Function. in: The Psychiatric Clinics of North America, Vol 18, No. 1. March 1995 pp 7 - 23.

180. Schreiner-Engel P: Female sexual arousability: its relation to gonadal hormones and the menstrual cycle. Diss Abst Int 41: 527, 1980.

181. Bancroft J, Sanders D, Davidson D, et al: Mood, sexuality, hormones and the menstrual cycle III. Sexuality and the role of androgens. Psychosom Med 1983; 45:509.

182. Waxenburg SE, Drellich MG, Sutherland AM: The role of hormones in human behavior. I: changes in female sexuality after adrenalectomy. J Clin Endocrinol Metab. 1959; 19:193.

183. Persky H, Lief HI, Strauss D, et al: Plasma testosterone level and sexual behavior in couples. Arch Sex Behav 1978; 7:157..

184. Udry JR, Talbert LM, Morris NM: Biosocial foundations for adolescent female sexuality. Demography 1986; 23:217.

185. Schreiner-Engel P, Schiavi RC, White D, et al: Low sexual desire in women: The role of reproductive hormones. Horm Behav 1989; 23:221.

186. Abplanalp JM, Rose RM, Donnelly AF, et al: Psychoendocrinology of the menstrual cycle II. The relationship between enjoyment of activities, moods and reproductive hormones. Psychosom Med 1979; 41:605.

187. Persky H, Charney N, Lief HI, et al: The relationship of plasma estradiol level to sexual behavior in young women. Psychosom Med 1978; 40:523.

188. Sherwin B: The psychoendocrinology of aging and female sexuality. Ann Review Sex Research 1991; 2:181.

189. Schreiner-Engel P, Schiavi RC, Smith H, et al: Sexual arousability and the menstrual cycle. Psychosom Med 1981; 43:199.

190. Meuwissen I, Over R: Sexual arousal across phases of the human menstrual cycle Arch Sex Behav 1992; 21:101.

191. Azadzoi KM, Tarcan T, Kim N, Siroky, M, Krane RJ, Goldstein I. Regulatory mechanism of clitoral, cavernosa, and vaginal smooth muscle contractility in the rabbit. J Urol 1998; 159, No. 5, Supplement, Abst. # 355.

192. Park K, Moreland RB, Atela A, Goldstein I, Traish A. Morphological/Biochemical characterization of human corpus clitoral smooth muscle cells in culture. J Urol 1998; 159, No. 5, Supplement, Abst. # 373.

193. deGroat WC, Booth AM: Physiology of male sexual function. Ann Intern Med 1980; 92:329.

194. Levin RJ: The mechanism of humane female sexual arousal. Annual Review of Sex Research 1992; 3:1.

195. Carmichael MS, Warburton VL, Dixen J, et al: Relationships among cardiovascular, muscular, and oxytocin responses during human sexual activity. Arch Sex Behav 1994; 23:59.

196. Heiman JR and Meston CM: Evaluating Sexual Dysfunction in Women. Clinical Obstetrics and Gynecology 1997; 40:No. 3:616-629.

197. Rosen RC, Taylor JF, Leiblum SR, et al. Prevalence of sexual dysfunction in women: results of a survey of 329 women in an

outpatient gynecological clinic. J Sex Marital Ther. 1993; 19:171-188.

198. Frank E, Anderson C, Rubenstein D. Frequency of sexual dysfunction in "normal" couples. N Engl J med. 1978; 299: 111-115.

199. Crenshaw TL, Goldberg JP. Sexual Pharmacology: Drugs that Affect Sexual Functioning. New York: WW Norton, 1996.

200. American Psychiatric Association. Diagnostic and Statistical Manual of Mental Disorders, 4th ed. Washington; American Psychiatric Association, 1994.

201. Meston CM, Gorzalka BB. Psychoactive drugs and human sexual behavior: The role of serotonergic activity. J Psychoactive Drugs. 1992; 24:1-40.

202. The Medical Letter, Inc. Drugs that cause sexual dysfunction: an update. Med Lett Drugs Ther 1992; 34:74-77.

203. Kaplan HS, Owen T. The female androgen deficiency syndrome. J Sex Marital Ther. 1993; 19:3-15.

204. Leiblum SR, Rosen RC, eds. Sexual Desire Disorders. New York: Guilford, 1988.

205. Heiman JR, LoPiccolo J. Becoming Orgasmic: A Sexual and Persoanl Growth Program for Women, 2nd ed. New York: Simon & Schuster, 1988.

206. Paavonen J: Vulvodynia - a complex syndrome of vulvar pain. Acta Obstet Gynecol Scand. 1995; 74:243-247.

207. Lynch PH: Vulvodynia: a syndrome of unexplained vulvar pain, psychologic disability and sexual dysfunction. J Reprod Med 1986; 31:773-80.

208. Goetsch MF: Vulvar vestibulitis. Prevalence and historical features in a general gynecologic practice population. Am J Obst Gynecol. 1991; 168:1609-16.

209. Marinoff SC, Turner MLC: Vulvar vestibulitis syndrome: An overview. Am J Obstet Gynecol 1991; 165:1228-33.

210. Pyka RE, Wilkinson EJ, Friedrich EG, Croker BP: The histopathology of vulvar vestibulitis syndrome. Int J Gynecol Pathol, 1988; 7:249-57

211. Woodruff JD, Fredrich EG: The vestibule. Clin Obstet Gynecol 1985; 28:134-41.

212. Friedrich EG: Vulvar vestibulitis syndrome. J Reprod Med 1987; 32:110-4.

213. Glazer HI, Rodke G, Swencionis C, Hertz R, and Young A: Treatment of vulvar vestibulitis syndrome with electromyographic biofeedback of pelvic floor musculature. J Reprod Med 1995; 40:283-90.

214. White G, Jantos A, Glazer H: Establishing the diagnosis of vulvar vestibulitis. J Reprod Med, 1997; 42:157-60.

215. Valins L. When a Woman's Body Says No to Sex: Understanding and Overcoming Vaginismus. New York: Penguin, 1992.

216. Bancroft J, Sanders D, Davidson DW, et al. Mood, sexuality, hormones and the menstrual cycle. III Sexuality and the role of androgens. Psychosom Med. 1983;45:509-516.

217 Sanders D, Warner P, Backstrom T, et al. Mood, sexuality, hormones and the menstrual cycle. I. Changes in mood and physical state: description of subjects and method. Psychosom Med. 1983; 45:487-501.

218. Alexander GM, Sherwin BB, Bancroft J, et al. Testosterone and sexual behaviors in oral contraceptive users and non-users, Horm Behav. 1990; 24:388-402.

219. Alexander GM, Sherwin BB, Sex steroids, sexual behavior, and selective attention for erotic stimuli in women using oral contraceptives. Psycho-neuroendocrinology. 1993; 18:91-102.

220. Robson KM, Brant HA, Kumar R. Maternal sexuality during first pregnancy and after childbirth. Br J Obstet Gynecol. 1981; 88:882-889.

221. Alder E, Bancroft J. The relationship between breast feeding persistence, sexuality and mood in post-partum women. Psychol Med. 1988; 18:389-396.

222. McCoy N, Davidson JM, A longitudinal study of the effects of menopause on sexuality. Maturitas. 1985; 7:203-210.

223. Meyers LS, Dixen J, Morreisette D, et al. Effects of estrogen, androgen, and progestin on psychophysiology and behavior in

post-menopausal women. J Clin Endocrinol Metab. 1990; 70:1124-1131.

224. Leiblum S, Bachman G, Kemmann E, et al. Vaginal atrophy in the post-menopausal women: the importance of sexual activity

225. Sherwin BB, Gelfand MM. The role of andogen in the maintenance of sexual functionig in oopherectomized women. Psychosom Med. 1987; 49:397-409.

226. Sherwin BB, Gelfand MM, Brender W. The role of androgen in the maintenance of sexual functioning in oopherectomized women. Psychosom Med. 1985; 47:339-351.

227. Sherwin B. The psychoendocrinology of aging and female sexuality. Ann Rev Sex Res. 1991; 21:181-199.

228. Pokras R, Hufinagel VC. Hysterectomies in the United States, 1965-1984. Vital and Health Statistics Series 13, No. 92 DHHS Publication No. (PHS) 87-1753. Hyattsville: National Center for Health Statistics, 1987.

229. Darling CA, McKay Smith YM. Understanding hysterectomies: Sexual satisaction and quality of life. J Sex Res. 1993; 30:324-335.

230. Bachmann GA, Psychosexual aspects of hysterectomy. Women's Health Issues. 1990; 1:41-49.

231. Carlson KJ, Miller BA, Fowler FJ. The Maine Women's Health Study: I. Outcomes of hysterectomy. Obstet Gynecol. 1994; 83:556-565.

232. American Cancer Society. Cancer facts and figures — 1994. Atlanta ACS, 1994.

233. Schain WS. Psychosocial factors in mastectomy and reconstruction. In: Noone AB, Decker BC, eds. Plastic and reconstructive sugery of the breast. Philadelphia: Decker, 1991; 327-343.

234. Clifford E. The reconstructive experience. The search for restitution. In: Georgiade NG, ed. Brest construction following mastectomy. St. Louis: CV Mosby, 1979:22-35.

235. Holland JC, Rowland JH. Patient rehabilitation and support. Psychosocial reactions to breast cancer and its treatment. In:

Harris JR, Hellman S, Henderson IC, Kinne DW, eds. Breast diseases. Philadelphia: JB Lippincott Co, 1987:632-647.

236. Rowland JH, Holland JC, Chaglassian T, Kinne D. Psychological response to breast reconstruction: expectations for and impact on post-mastectomy functioning. Psychosomatics 1993; 34:241-250.

237. Maas P, Brown SE, and Bruning N: The Mend Clinic Guide to Natural Medicine for Menopause and Beyond. New York, Dell Publishing, 1997, 208-238.

Support Groups and Other Helpful Organizations

Many fine organizations support men with impotence and other urological problems, such as prostate cancer. Listed below are major national organizations that can put one in touch with local support groups and other resources in your area. This first group includes organizations either for the advancement of urological diseases in general or for impotence specifically.

American Foundation for Urologic Disease (AFUD)
>   The latest information on prostate cancer, new research and clinical applications is available.
>   300 W. Pratt St., Ste. 401
>   Baltimore, MD 21201
>   1-800-242-2383

Geddings Osbon Foundations
>   Information and a booklet on impotence, primarily focusing on vacuum erection devices, but reviewing all options. Impotence education, services and support.
>   PO Box 1593
>   Augusta, GA 30903-1593
>   1-800-433-4215

Sex Information and Education Council of the U.S.
>   Provides literature on sexuality and illness.
>   130 W. 42nd St.
>   New York, NY 10036
>   1-212-819-9770

Impotence Institute of America
>   Information on impotence problems resulting from prostate cancer treatment or any other cause.
>   10400 Little Patuxent Parkway, Suite 485
>   Columbia, MD 21044-3502
>   1-800-669-1603

American Urological Association (AUA)
>   1120 North Charles St.
>   Baltimore, MD 21201-5559
>   (410) 727-1100

Impotence Resource Center
>   PO Box 1593
>   Augusta, GA 30903

National Kidney and Urologic Disease Information Clearinghouse
>   For information on BPH and its treatment.
>   Box NKUDIC
>   9000 Rockville Pike
>   Bethesda, MD 20892
>   (301) 654-4415

This next group of organizations includes support groups and organizations that provide information for men with cancer and other diseases, such as Parkinson's disease where impotence is frequently a side effect of the disease or the treatment of the disease. These organizations also will be helpful in putting you in touch with support groups in your area and other resources in your area.

American Cancer Society

A voluntary health organization offering a wide variety of free services and literature to patients and their families. Literature is available on all cancers, nutrition, dealing with stress and anxiety, plus legal and financial planning. Some chapters provide transportation (or can refer you) if needed, information regarding support groups, and a range of other helpful services locally. The society is also involved in funding scientific research and community education. Find a local chapter in the telephone book or contact the national office at:

1599 Clifton Road DE
Atlanta, GA 30329-4251
1-800-227-2345

National Cancer Institute (NCI)

The NCI provides written material and information on a variety of cancer-related topics, and it makes referrals to local and regional cancer-treatment centers.

Office of Cancer Communications National Cancer Institute
31 Center Drive MSC 2580
Building 31 Room 10A16
Bethesda, MD 20892-2580

The Cancer Information Service

A nationwide telephone service for cancer patients and their families, as well as the general public and health care professionals, that answers questions and provides free booklets about cancer.

1-800-4-CANCER (1-800-422-6237)

CancerFax

Provides treatment summaries, with current data on prognosis, relevant staging and histologic classifications, news and announcements of important cancer-related issues.

(301) 402-5874 (fax)

Prostate Cancer Support Group Network (PCSN)

This is one of the leading nationwide prostate-cancer support networks, pursuing government advocacy issues, financing research and focusing on increasing public awareness of prostate cancer.

300 W. Pratt St., Ste. 401
Baltimore, MD 21201
1-800-828-7866

US-TOO

One of the largest patient-organized support groups: focuses on survivor support and offers fellowship and counseling. Provides prostate-cancer survivors and their families with emotional and educational support through an international network of support groups and a quarterly newsletter.

930 N. Yord Rd., Ste. 50
Hinsdale, IL 60521-2993
1-708-323-1002
(800) 808-7866
(630) 323-1002
(630) 323-1003 (fax)

Cancer Care, Inc.

Provides free professional counseling, support groups and educational materials.

1180 Avenue of the Americas
New York, NY 10036
(800) 813-HOPE
(212) 302-2400
(212) 719-0263 (fax)

CaP Cure

1250 Fourth St., Suite 360
Santa Monica, Calif. 90401

(310) 458-2873
Fax (301) 458-8074

**National Institute on Aging
Information Center**
PO Box 8057
Gaithersburg, MD 20898-8057
(800) 222-2225

U.S. Food and Drug Administration (FDA)
Drug Information Branch
5600 Fishers Lane
Rockville, MD 20857
(301) 827-4573

National Parkinson Foundation, Inc.
1501 NW 9th Ave.
Miami, FL 33136
1-800-327-4545 (Canada and
U.S., except FL and CA)
1-800-433-7022 (FL)
1-800-400-8448 (CA)

This last group of organizations includes support groups and organizations that provide information for women with breast cancer.

"Encore Plus"—A program of YWCA of the USA
"Encore Plus" is for women over 50 in need of early cancer detection information, breast and cervical cancer screening, or support services. Other services include peer-group support and exercise programs.
624 9th Street, NW, 3rd Floor
Washington, DC 20001-5394
202-628-3636
hn2202@handsnet.org

Mothers Supporting Daughters with Breast Cancer
MSDBC helps women whose daughters have breast cancer, so they can better help their daughters cope with the disease and treatment. Call for info and handbook.
21710 Bayshore Road
Chestertown, MD 21620-4401
410-778-1982
lilliepie@aol.com

National Alliance of Breast Cancer Organizations
A non-profit agency representing some 300 organizations concerned about breast cancer. Services include physician referrals, job discrimination-related advocacy, professional education, and a speaker's bureau.
9 East 37th Street, 10th Floor
New York, NY 10016
800-719-9154
nabcoinfo@aol.com

National Breast Cancer Coalition
A grassroots advocacy group of more than 300 member organizations and thousands of individuals dedicated to the eradication of breast cancer through action, advocacy, and public education.
1707 L Street, NW, Suite 1060
Washington, DC 20036
202-296-7477
www.natlbcc.org

Susan G. Komen Breast Cancer Foundation
Dedicated to eradicating breast cancer through research, education, screening, and treatment. Services include research and program grants and a toll-freee "Helpline" staffed by trained volunteers.
5005 LBJ Freeway, Suite 370
Dallas, TX 75244
214-450-1777
800-IM-AWARE

Index

About the Author

DR. AL NEWMAN is one of the nation's leading urologists and has been treating men with impotence problems for two decades. Married and the father of two children, he lives and practices in Montgomery, Alabama. He holds B.S. and Ph.D. degrees in chemistry from the University of Alabama, an M.D. from the University of South Alabama, and was a post-doctoral fellow at the University of Alabama-Birmingham. He did his urology training at Baylor College of Medicine in Houston, Texas, where he worked with Dr. Brantley Scott, inventor of the penile implants used today. Dr. Newman is one of fifteen urologists now participating in a national FDA study on penile prostheses and is also conducting a double-blind study on the role of Viagra with patients who already have penile implants. In 1984, he started "Potency Restored of Montgomery," one of the longest-running impotence support groups in the U.S., with many couples still in attendance who first attended in the mid-1980s. In his spare time, and with his wife, Carolyn, he is an avid collector of art.